Get Rich as a Woman

3 Proven Ways to Make Yourself a Millionaire

D1714519

Lauralee Swift

Table of Contents

Introduction

There has never been a time in history when women, including you, have had such realistic and attainable opportunities to make themselves rich. This partly explains why approximately 33% of the millionaires in the U.S. are women (McCain, 2022). You can't afford to let such a chance pass you by, and you'll regret it later if you don't grab your opportunity by the horns. Now is your moment.

No one likes being poor. Women desire to be able to fend for themselves and their loved ones without feeling vulnerable or used, as these feelings can lead to a sense of inferiority, low self-esteem, and even depression. Some cases of the inferiority complex in women are due to inadequate finances. Some end up being taken advantage of because they do not have enough money to live life the way they want. If any of these relate to you, then you are in the right place—this book is for you. Could it be that you have a nine-to-five job but still feel like you are going round and round in circles, without growing any wealth? Have you been searching for ways to escape the rat race that is associated with long hours but to no avail? If that is the case, your search is over, because this book will guide you to the world of rich women.

Many people picture themselves winning the lottery or doing other things that make them rich overnight. The hustle and bustle all around is that of people just trying to keep their heads above water, or those trying to prepare themselves for retirement.

For most women, money is an intimidating subject. Many women allow fear to hold them back and deter them from working toward their goals. However, there are also women who are striving toward getting rich and are conscious of every action they take in trying to achieve these goals. Everything good in life (getting rich included) takes careful planning and determination. Of course, what worked for one might not work for you, but what is important is that you find your own trajectory and your own success story!

Get Rich as a Woman introduces three strategies that will help you realize your dream of becoming rich. These three strategies have been proven to work because they are pillars to the success of about 88% of millionaires, all of whom are self-made (Lisa, 2022). I am very excited about this transformational book, which will help get you up on your feet and ready to make the bold move to start getting rich. The three strategies, which are named "The Train," "The Plane," and "The Rocket," are explained fully, and you can make a choice of which method or combination works best for you. You will also learn a lot of key factors to getting rich, which include believing in yourself, defining the motive for getting rich, and how best to achieve your goal through your chosen strategy.

As you read through this book, your mindset will gradually change to match that of building and maintaining wealth. Here are some of the changes that you should expect as you read on:

- You will begin to see the possibility and reality of achieving your dream of financial success.

- You will realize that your situation is not necessarily a barrier to getting to your goal.

- You will attain the confidence to take the necessary steps to success.

In a world that is slowly moving away from being sexist when it comes to equal opportunities, women still have a lot more work to do to get themselves out there. It is a good thing that women are beginning to seize their independence and become powerful forces to be reckoned with in the business world. Women are becoming masters at money management and are shifting their mindsets from the prehistoric assumption that the best way for a woman to get rich is to marry rich. This is the perfect time for you to start on your journey of getting rich.

This book is carefully structured to be a companion on your journey to success. The strategies described here, if adopted and applied correctly, will help you navigate your way in the business world. Having read this book, you will realize that you are ready to make the bold moves that are key to getting rich. You will learn a lot of things that can contribute to your success. Experience is often said to be the best teacher, and yes, the experience can be yours or others. I will introduce you to practical examples of other women who have grown their own wealth.

One thing I would love for my readers to embrace is that getting rich stretches far beyond a dollar amount. It is important to understand that being rich is a state of mind. When you understand this, you will realize that in the same sense that you desire to be successful financially, you should also desire to live an enriching life. These two go hand in hand, and richness that is a combination of both is more wholesome and satisfying. I hope that you will have a great read, and I am sure that this book is just what you need for the mindset shift that will help you to achieve your goal of getting rich.

Happy journeys on your way to becoming a female millionaire!

Chapter 1:

What Does It Mean to "Be Rich"?

First things first—this book is all about how to get rich financially. However, we would be remiss if we don't talk about what being "truly rich" really means, considering that it is a lot more than just the money itself. This chapter will unleash the fact that there are different meanings of "being rich." You'll also learn how being rich doesn't just mean accumulating more money—there is more to the equation. Money isn't the ultimate end goal, but it is necessary to secure some comforts and tools that will aid your satisfaction and that of others.

"Being Rich" Redefined

One can be "rich" spiritually, emotionally, and relationally, but the focus of this book is indeed how to become rich financially. However, when becoming rich financially, it is vital that you create and maintain a "balance" so that other major areas of your life are not negatively affected. This means that as the money in your bank account and wallet increases, keeping your relationships as well as your spiritual, physical, and emotional lives rich is also of paramount importance. In fact, your financial riches should improve all the other areas of your life.

When you become richer financially, you'll have all those other categories of your life that you can pour your finances into. These include your family, your health and relationships, and don't forget helping other people. You will be in a position where you're "financially strong" and able to stand on your own two feet. This way, you will be in a position to help others around you. After all, money isn't important in and of itself. Rather, it is how you can use that money—how it can serve yourself and others. This is where the ultimate "richness" will come from, certainly not from the money itself. With this in mind, we will explore some ways through which you can use your money to enrich other areas of your life. This will help you prepare to use your money to attain complete satisfaction once you get rich financially.

Spiritual Enrichment

True satisfaction in life is supported by spiritual enrichment. Therefore, directing your riches toward improving your spiritual position is a noble cause. Often, women fear life's responsibilities because they feel they don't have what it takes to tackle them, especially financially. Waking up to a new morning can be a nightmare when you are financially unstable. Therefore, the money that you accumulate over time should enable you to live in confidence, without the fear of facing everyday responsibilities. This, in turn, enhances your personal spiritual life.

You will realize that the relationship between your spiritual life and money is mainly reflected in three aspects, which are gratitude, generosity, and trust. These factors put your money to work in the spiritual sense; I will explain in this section.

Trust Yourself

Have you ever felt like you simply can't trust yourself with money? Do you simply feel that you cannot effectively use the money to trigger relevant and positive changes in yourself and others? Becoming financially rich should boost the confidence and trust that you have in yourself with regard to money and other issues. This is a crucial part of becoming financially secure. As your money grows, also work on believing in yourself. This is not a one-day event, but self-trust can grow over time once good habits have been put in place.

Please note that even if you have billions in your bank account, there are some things that you simply can't solve with money. Trust also involves settling into a feeling of ease even when you face such circumstances. Simply accept what you cannot change and trust yourself. Develop and preserve self-trust.

Be Generous

Generosity can be described as one's willingness to be a "giving" person. This could be giving to members of your family who are in need or engaging in being generous to community organizations. You feel fulfilled when you are willing and able to give your energy, time, and money.

It is important to remember that your generosity should remain within your means and ability. There is no point in being generous at the cost of yourself because you won't derive satisfaction from the practice. Even as more money becomes available to you, remember that financial contributions are not the only way to show generosity. You can still give mentorship, support, and time. If there are any noble causes that you can participate in, please do so to the best of your ability.

Gratitude

It is surprising how, as humans, we often find it difficult to appreciate what we have. Instead, we tend to concentrate on what isn't available to us, and that's a reflection of a lack of gratitude. Being thankful is a crucial aspect of life fulfillment, and your money should help you to cultivate that attitude. Resist the urge to become greedy because this will not only make you spiritually numb but will also nurture insensitivity toward other human beings.

Take some time to look at what you have achieved in your life so far. Pause a moment and appreciate where you came from. Be grateful for every good event and improvement in your life. Be thankful that you can afford what you couldn't two, five, or ten years ago.

Relational Enrichment

While people can still cultivate relationships with the people around them even when there isn't much money around, having it can make a huge difference if used correctly. In meaningful relationships that you already have, your higher financial status should be like a glue that makes the relationship stronger. You can even establish completely new connections when you have money.

We cannot deny the fact that there are some connections that are difficult to have when you don't have money. Under such circumstances, doors seem closed when you don't have what it takes financially to be in that relationship. For example, your money should help you to establish some strong business relationships where you have to put something on the table, especially financially. You can even enter into certain partnerships that you probably couldn't previously, when you didn't have the money. If used wisely, money can also improve the relationships that you have with the people who are close to you, like your partner, family, and friends.

The Psychology of Money and Relationships

In this book, we encourage you to do everything possible to help ensure that your relationships improve as the money you have increases. However, you should understand the impact that money usually has on relationships, according to psychology. Some say, "To be fore-warned is to be fore-armed," so understanding these concepts will help you to work toward better relationships. Here are two theories that point out some important facts about money and relationships:

- **The social or economic exchange theory (Langabeer, 2022)**: This theory suggests that money is used either as a reward or punishment in relationships. As a result, money triggers feelings of fear, anxiety, and insecurity in some parties involved in relationships.

Therefore, you don't want your money to be a threat to the people around you, though sometimes there isn't much you can do about that. Do everything possible to make others feel secure around you.

- **The evolutionary psychology perspective (Psychology Today, 2019)**: According to this theory, money is linked to security and survival. This means that when people do not have money, they may feel insecure about their livelihoods around you. You are more likely to meet people who will feel insecure because their financial reserves are depleted. If your resources permit, you can help them regain their sense of security and survival. While some might need help with just a few dollars, others may need assistance to start some projects that could generate income for them.

Emotional Enrichment

One study reported that the emotional health of many Americans gets better as their income levels increase until it reaches a plateau (Kahneman & Deaton, 2010). According to the study, this plateau is reached when people begin to earn about $75,000. At this stage, there may not be much change in emotional well-being. Therefore, you should allow your emotional health to become more stable as you grow financially.

There are various strategies that you can put in place to ensure that your money is supportive of your mental well-being, and these include

- investing in vacations and time out.
- surrounding yourself with like-minded people.

- attending conferences and meetings that focus on well-being.

- resting and getting enough sleep.

Social Enrichment

No matter how much money you have, you still have social obligations as a human being. You still have to exhibit a humane nature that is laced with empathy and love toward others. Results from an interesting study reported that less expensive cars were more likely to allow pedestrians to pass on crosswalks than luxury cars (Anwar, 2012). The same study also revealed that luxury car drivers tend to cut off other fellow drivers on the road. The researchers extrapolated that this could be because being wealthy is associated with the feeling of entitlement that somehow belittles others. You should aim to be among the minority who still respect others and their rights, irrespective of the amount of money that you have.

You can also consider giving generously. Orphanages and seniors' homes are possible places where your assistance will be much appreciated in your community. Always find ways to "pay it forward" and put a smile on another person's face. Sometimes, you don't have to give someone money, as just showing them love goes a long way. Cultivate and practice empathy, and you will be surprised to see that your money is there to make your life better without the need to thwart others in the process.

Physical Enrichment

Sometimes, being able to afford so much can be a problem if you don't discipline yourself with regard to your lifestyle. For example, you might be able to afford all the junk food in the world, but it takes discipline to create and stick to certain boundaries for you to live longer and stay healthy. You need to be healthy to enjoy your money and be available for others as well. There are three major practices that will contribute to your health, and these are your diet, physical activity, and sleep.

Diet

Learn to eat a balanced diet with appropriate amounts of carbohydrates, proteins, fats, and other micronutrients. It is recommended that you include plant-based foods in your diet as much as you can. Even though you can afford to eat in restaurants, cooking at home is usually better, as you can use healthier methods of preparing your food.

Physical Activity

Exercise also helps to keep your body healthy. Here are some of the benefits that exercise can give you, contributing to your overall health:

- It makes your muscles and bones strong.

- It improves brain functions that are related to memory, thinking, and balance.

- It can be a vital tool for managing your weight.

- It boosts your energy levels.

- It lowers stress, depression, and anxiety.

- It can reduce uncontrolled appetite.

- Its effects are protective against chronic diseases such as diabetes and heart disease.

- It lowers blood pressure to normal levels.

You can engage in different forms of exercise and still enjoy the benefits. These could be strength, stretch, or cardiovascular workouts. Strength exercises usually involve weightlifting like dumbbells and barbells or doing squats and push-ups. Cardiovascular workouts increase your heart and breathing rates. Jogging, walking, cycling, and jump-rope are all examples of cardiovascular exercises that you can do.

Sleep

Both the quality and quantity of your sleep matter. The quality of your sleep refers to how deep you can sleep, while the quantity describes the amount of time that you take to sleep. For adults, it is recommended that you sleep for at least seven hours a night (Olson, 2021). Please note that sleeping too much is also not a good idea, which is why some experts suggest a maximum of nine hours of quality sleep (Roland, 2022).

Are you wondering what good sleep might really contribute to your health? There are plenty of benefits, and these include

- stress reduction and an improved mood.

- helping you to maintain a healthy weight.

- lowered risk of health issues like heart disease and diabetes.

- improving the way your brain functions.

Future Enrichment

When you are financially rich, you also want to think about the future. Consider investing so that you remain financially secure even when you are no longer able to work and make more money. If you have children, you could teach them your business and money-making ventures so that they can take over when you become incapable or are ready to retire. This kind of forethought can shape a bright future for generations to come.

The Rich Mindset

Please note that the "rich mindset" has nothing to do with financial status. It's possible for a "poor" person to have a rich mindset, even when they don't have many financial resources. The danger comes when a rich person has a "poor mindset," as this can affect the way they use their wealth in negative ways. This is partly why we compiled the information in this section to assist you to adopt a "rich mindset" as you prepare to accumulate wealth.

A rich mindset is one that does not only focus on having a surplus but also on using it to accelerate other things such as education, business, as well as social and personal relationships. Simply put, all the different forms of enrichment that we explained in this chapter are driven by a "rich mindset." On the contrary, a "poor mindset" has no long-term perceptions of surplus. It concentrates on consumption. To help you further understand the "rich mindset" so that you can work on adopting it, let's highlight the factors that differentiate it from the "poor mindset."

- **Learning**: The rich mindset is more susceptible to learning. People with this kind of mindset believe that they don't know everything, which is why they are ready to get new and corrected information from various sources, including other people. As a "rich woman," you can use your wealth to further your knowledge or you can help others to do so. A poor mindset thinks that they know it all so there is nothing more to learn. Remember, to them, getting more money is the destination, yet they refuse to do what is needed to get there.

- **Relationships**: When you have a rich mindset, building authentic relationships is one of your core values. You don't use your money to manipulate others for your sole personal benefit. The relationships that are formed using a rich mindset are hinged on attributes such as trust, mutual respect, and common values. A rich mindset appreciates that it is possible and noble to do something for other people, even if they don't give you anything in return. This is contrary to the "I scratch your back, you scratch mine" kind of mindset that is reflected by those with poor mindsets.

- **Investment**: Investment is not all about putting in or getting money. You can invest your time, energy, and resources and still gain great personal satisfaction in return. This is the kind of perspective that helps people with rich mindsets to offer their time and other resources to meet the needs of their friends and communities. They can be content with the feeling of satisfaction that they get upon engaging in social and charitable activities. Well, a poor mindset will think otherwise. It focuses on short-term, money-related returns. A poor mindset believes that every hour spent should have some dollar returns attached to it.

- **View on other people's success**: People with a rich mindset are truly happy when others do well. They derive encouragement from others' achievements and are challenged to do better. People with poor mindsets feel that the success of another person further limits resources, thereby making it difficult for them to also make it. They let bitterness, hatred, and jealousy get the best of them, stealing their joy and leaving them unfulfilled. When you have this type of mindset, you might not get the urge to help others even when you have all the resources at your disposal.

- **Reputation**: To a person with a rich mindset, reputation is important. This is one of the reasons why they will do what is needed to embody a behavior that is acceptable, socially or otherwise. No matter how much money you have, you never should depend on bribes to get things done if you have a rich mindset. People with poor mindsets try to derail authentic procedures of doing things and use their resources to manipulate others.

- **The need for one another**: Money cannot keep you company, wash your dishes, clean your house, water your garden, or run errands for you, but other people can. It is only a rich mindset that realizes the fact that one cannot do everything all by themself. We all need one another for our world to go around, so there is no point in underrating someone's presence, even if they do not have as much money as you have. With a rich mindset, you will understand that there are core strengths that you can focus on while you let others assist, as you can't do everything. Unlike this type of mindset, the poor mindset believes that doing everything is possible as long as you work hard.

- **Quitting**: People with rich mindsets do quit, too, but only in a well-calculated manner. They strategically plan to quit after seeing that, say, there aren't enough resources to complete given tasks. They would save the available resources rather than staying on a sinking ship. Someone with a poor mindset would quit as an impromptu reaction to situations and pain, acting out of feelings instead of making a decision based on facts.

Activity

Below is a table that requires you to explain what *you* mean by "getting rich." Write as much as you can and read it to yourself. If you are comfortable, you can also find someone to read what you wrote and ask them to tell you their thoughts.

Question	What do you understand by the phrase "getting rich"?
Answer	

This chapter has emphasized the fact that getting rich is far beyond just accumulating a lot of money. It encompasses the social, physical, emotional, relational, and spiritual aspects of life. In fact, the million-dollar question would be: "What will I do with the money that I gather?" or "How will my money impact the social, relational, emotional, and other areas of my life?" If it will have positive effects on any of these, then, according to this book, you are "truly rich." We also highlighted that you need a "rich mindset" to experience what "being rich" is like. Now that you understand what being rich is, it's time to determine the reason why you want to experience financial abundance. Find out more about this in the next chapter.

Chapter 2:

What Is Your "Why"?

Your "why" is your superpower that will let you sail through the many obstacles you will face on your journey to getting rich. Getting rich is not all that "complicated"—it is actually somewhat "simple" if you follow the tried and proven steps. While getting rich is quite simple, it is not "easy"—which is true of almost anything that is worth doing in life. The fact that getting rich is not easy partly explains why you absolutely need to know your "why." You will come across some obstacles along the way, and if you don't know your "why," which is your true motivation, then the likelihood of quitting when the road gets bumpy and things get hard is high. You can't just say "I want to be rich" without a solid reason(s) for why you strongly desire that to happen. Therefore, by helping you realize your "why," this chapter will motivate you to complete this book along with the steps that are presented throughout.

The Key Next Step: Pinpoint the "Why"

Do you already know why you want to be rich? Whatever your reason might be, that is what will keep you focused on your money-making goal, even when the going gets tougher. If you are not yet aware of the reasons why you intend to get rich, we will take you through some ideas that will help you find your "why." Please note that it is also possible to update your "why make money" trigger, so even if you have some reasons that you are already aware of, going through this section will help you. There are two main ways through which you can identify your "whys" with regard to getting rich. First, you can pinpoint your *pains,* and second, you can determine your *goals.* Therefore, the ideas that we will outline in this section will be hinged on these two main points.

Determine Your Goals

Sometimes, your push to make money might be because the goals that you have in life require financial abundance for them to be achievable. What is something that you have always wanted to do but couldn't do because you didn't have enough money? Identifying those particular goals or objectives could be all you need to determine your reasons for pursuing wealth.

Trust the Process

Maybe you don't know what your goals are. Here are some steps that you can follow to come up with actionable wealth goals:

1. Get a notebook and pen. Sit in a quiet place so that you can focus.

2. On one page of your notebook, create two columns, one labeled "long-term" and the other "short-term." Think deeply and write down wealth goals that fall under each of the two categories.

3. Analyze all the points that you have noted down and see if there are any main themes that are emerging. Identify goals that have deeper meanings, such as, "I want to take proper care of my family" or "I intend to travel at least

once a year." Such goals are the ones that reflect your "why." Some, like the ones that only mention how much money you intend to raise, are also good wealth goals, but they don't lead you to your "why."

4. On another page and in a larger font, write down the "whys" that are emphasized by the themes that you noticed in the goals that you listed above.

Ideas for Good Wealth Goals

It's brainstorming time! Let's go through some ideas that might open your eyes to the goals that can help you find your "why."

- **Taking good care of parents**: You might want to be in a better position to take care of your parents and improve their way of living. Perhaps your goal is to accumulate enough wealth to allow your parents to rest during their retirement so that they won't end up having to work when they are no longer physically or mentally up to it. You probably just want to make your parents proud so they see that the hard work they put into you was not in vain.

- **Better lifestyle**: You might not be suffering, but there is a lifestyle that you simply wish you could live. Could it be that you prefer living in a bigger house with more rooms, even though the one you are currently living in is standard and good enough? Maybe you just want to be able to afford different things, no matter their price. If you are always admiring certain lifestyles of others that are associated with more wealth, then a lifestyle change might be your goal.

- **Increasing the leverage to follow your passions**: Are there things that you are doing now just for the sake of money? It could be a job, sport, connection, and so on. I'm talking of those things that make you say, "If it wasn't for the fact that I don't have enough money, I would never go for this." If you sometimes find yourself thinking along those lines, then you might want to make more money so that you can follow your true passions.

- **Maintaining connections**: There might be times when you miss certain people in your life, not because they are no more but due to the fact that they are too far from your reach. Money is probably all you need to be able to travel to them or rather have them come to you. So, if your desire is to maintain physical connections despite the distance, reflect deeply and see if this could be your wealth goal.

- **Leaving a nine-to-five job**: The rat race that is associated with nine-to-five jobs can be really frustrating at times. The routines and lack of freedom involved can be tiring. When getting rich seems like the only way to break off from this situation, you certainly push for it.

- **Improving your personal health**: With enough money, you can see the relevant specialists when you need to. For example, you can afford to approach a nutritionist, something that you wouldn't do when your funds are limited. You can even afford healthy, expensive food. Sometimes, the reason why people go for unhealthy fast foods is that they are cheaper. There are so many gadgets that enhance better health, but they can only be afforded by the rich. Think of the blue light-blocking sunglasses, water ionizers, and red light therapy devices—amazing health-oriented tools require a lot of money. There is no doubt that when you want this upper-level access to health, you will need to be rich.

- **Having a global impact**: Significant moves that attract global attention are usually possible for the wealthy. For instance, you could invest your money into a novel technological idea that might positively impact the whole world. If your desire is to be involved in something that will change the world, money can easily get you there, hence the need to get rich.

- **Owning your time**: When you don't have much money, you rarely own your time. Rather, your time is owned by those who give you the money that you use to earn a living. When you have won money, you can spend your time the way you want, and you can enjoy life better that way.

- **Increased exposure**: Getting rich is a door to knowing so many things. You can travel and learn from various cultures. You become less scared to approach certain people, so you connect with people who have strategic positions in organizations. The list is endless, but in essence, being wealthy exposes you to better opportunities and associations.

Identifying Your Pain

Have you ever faced situations in life where you think, "If only I had money..."? Such scenarios are a true reflection of the pains that can motivate you to do whatever it takes to earn money and get rich. You will work hard just to avoid getting back into that particular situation again. This section will enlighten you on some pains that you might use as your "whys."

- **Experiencing intense lack**: If you ever went through periods when you lacked even the basic needs, you might feel the urge to get rich and help other people in similar scenarios. Lots of charity organizations were founded that way. This is reason enough to push you toward achieving the goal of getting rich.

- **Tired of dependence**: Depending on other people for everything that you want to do can be a pain. It is the desire of nearly every human being to be able to do things without having to wait for someone else to come and make things happen. Being tired of being on the "asking" side all the time can trigger the need to get rich.

- **Tired of abuse**: Various forms of abuse can make people feel unwanted, irrelevant, or unheard. It makes people victims of an inferiority complex. This can trigger the desire to get rich in a bid to feel important and worthy and to gain some respect.

- **Helping a sick or disadvantaged loved one**: There are some people who are in the pharmaceutical research industry not just because they really love discovering remedies for certain diseases. Some have painful stories of how they lost their loved ones to certain diseases while they were not in a good position to help. The same feelings apply when lack of money is the only barrier hindering the success, happiness, or health of your loved one. This might then motivate you to get rich and turn things around for the people you love.

- **The past experience of an inferiority complex**: Sometimes, the inadequacy that comes with being poor may promote the development of an inferiority complex in an individual. Having an inferiority complex makes life unbearable because it makes you feel out of place under various circumstances. You might just feel that everyone else is better than you for some reason. Other people tend to be better positioned to accomplish things than you are. Instead of dwelling in the negative effects of the inferiority complex, you could take your situation as a motivation to work toward getting rich.

- **Insecurity about the future**: It's so difficult to wake up each day not knowing where you will get your next meal, not because there are too many options but due to unavailability of resources, especially money. We all want the peace that comes with being more secure about the next day, week, month, or year. Therefore, this is enough reason for you to desire to be rich.

The Summary of It All

As much as you might have many personalized ideas about the reasons why you might need to get rich, you will realize that they all fall into at least one of the categories that we will highlight in this section. These are

- **Status**: We cannot underestimate the power of higher status. Richard Templar once highlighted that status makes you a target of prestigious invitations and connections to important people in remarkable positions (Sara, 2018). Who doesn't want such a privilege?

- **Security**: It is the desire of every human being to live a life where they are not worried by issues such as food, shelter, health, and so on. In essence, everyone wants to feel secure and safe.

- **Influence**: People want their views to be heard or considered. We all desire to be listened to, and for some reason, people respect the ideas of those who have more money. So, you might aim to get more money so that you can exert influence.

- **Charity**: People who are more oriented toward making the globe a better place for others will certainly need money to pursue that cause. Therefore, charity is one of the reasons why you might work hard to become rich.

- **Comfort**: In addition to having major needs such as food and shelter covered, human beings cherish lives that are more comfortable. For example, instead of just having any shelter over your head, you might desire a bigger, spacious, and well-furnished home. While having food on your table might be good, the ability to eat exactly what you want at any given time is an extra step that requires more wealth.

- **Leisure**: Sometimes, you just need to do things that require less work and are more relaxing and pleasurable. Traveling, meeting new people, playing games, and attending pleasurable events are all part of leisure. Unless you have some extra dollars to spare, you cannot go for leisure.

- **Luxury**: Luxury has more to do with wants; that is, things that you don't really need for survival. For example, you can eat good food at your house or a less expensive restaurant, but you might just decide to have your dinner at a luxurious hotel. That calls for a wealthy pocket.

- **Freedom:** Imagine a life where you own your time, money, and yourself—that's freedom. When you don't have enough money, your next step depends on the decisions of other people who seem to fuel your livelihood. The desire to break free and earn freedom could be your sole motivation for wanting to get rich.

- **Mobility**: If you are a travel fanatic who is only limited by funds, then mobility could be your "why." Moving between towns, cities, countries, or even continents is a money-oriented venture.

- **Popularity**: Being well off can make you popular; that is, people will like you. They could like you for what you can offer, but the fact still remains that you become popular with money. So, getting rich is one of the easiest ways to earn popularity.

The Key Action

Using the ideas that you learned from this chapter, it's time to focus and determine why you want to become rich. Once you have your "why," write it on a card—it could be an index card or something similar. Please note that it is fine to have more than one reason why you want to get rich, just write them down on the card. When you write your "whys," be sure to connect them with the phrase "so that." For example, you could write:

- **Question:** Why do I want to be rich?

- **Answer:** I want to be rich *so that* I can live a more comfortable life and travel the world.

Ideally, place your card where you can see it every day. Also, be sure to read it aloud every single day as a way of reminding yourself that you have a serious task ahead of you while encouraging yourself to move forward.

Chapter 3:

What Are Your "Why Nots"?

According to Henry Ford, "Obstacles are those frightful things you see when you take your eyes off your goal." In the previous chapter, we emphasized that your goal can be your motivation, so once you lose your focus on it, you become prone to obstacles, circumstances, and situations that will make you feel like you might not be able to achieve your goals. Simply put, your goal is your "why" while the obstacles that you come across along the way are your "why nots."

In this chapter, the focus is on the "why nots." Highlighting the various obstacles that might come your way will give you a heads-up that will help you to tackle them in healthy and effective ways. Some of the "why nots" could be negative things that you believe or have been telling yourself, which nurture the notion that you can't succeed in this endeavor. Therefore, this chapter aims to reassure you that you should never view obstacles as blockers to your destiny. It will encourage you to develop a "conqueror mindset" that will also foster the "money-making" one that you probably have already.

Some "Why Nots" to Conquer

Reaching your financial goals will help you to deal with some of your pains and enjoy the lifestyle that you have always desired.

In this section, we will highlight some of the obstacles that might come your way and possible strategies for dealing with them. We will categorize these obstacles into three groups, which are general, mental, and thought-related obstacles.

General

In this category, we will discuss obstacles that do not specifically relate to mental and thought-related obstacles. Let's get down to it.

Time Constraints

Time can be a serious constraint, especially when you have a nine-to-five job that you are committed to. Under such circumstances, you might find it difficult to create enough time to work toward your goal of getting rich. By the time you knock off from work, you are probably too tired to chase some of the objectives that connect to your goal. Well, that's how it is, but you will need to find strategies to get around this issue because you still want to get rich, right? Here are some practical ideas:

- **Find your way around distractions**: If you have ever worked in a shared office, you will understand how such a working environment can distract you from your work. Apart from having one colleague after another stopping by your desk for a chat, your phone rings constantly and you have to attend to it. If you are working on a computer, an interesting ad pops up and you find yourself spending the next 30 minutes following through several links to get more information on it. If you are to take all these and other aspects into account, you will note that you often lose a considerable amount of time in your day. So, it's not like you don't have the time, but some of the bulk of it is stolen by distraction. Identify what derails your attention from your tasks and do everything possible to manage it. For example, when you are working on a certain task, you could simply train yourself not to click on any ad, no matter how interesting. Taking out avoidable distractions will leave you with more time to channel toward your endeavors to get rich.

- **Create the time**: If time seems to be unavailable, create it. For example, if your day is clogged with other activities that contribute to your current lifestyle, then sacrificing part of your evening might be the way to go. It's true that sleeping about eight hours a day is highly recommended, but there are times when you have no better option than to break the rule. Did you know that some millionaires that you emulate today sleep only for a few hours, just enough to get them rejuvenated to make money? Think of Elon Musk, who is the CEO of SpaceX and Tesla. Musk's sleeping routine is from 1 a.m. to 7 a.m., which is a six-hour stretch (Merle, 2017). Barack Obama, the former U.S. President, also follows a similar routine. Many others, including Tim Armstrong, the CEO of AOL, and Richard Branson, who founded Virgin Group, also sleep for about six hours at night but are still making it. You can also adjust your sleeping patterns to create more time for your money-making goals.

- **Assign other tasks**: Sometimes, the reason why time might be an issue could be because you simply have too many responsibilities on your shoulders. Delegating some duties to others can help in such cases. Assigning tasks to other people can create more time during which you can pursue your money-making goals.

Lack of Skills

Getting rich involves excelling in a certain area or industry, but that can be a challenge when you don't have the relevant skills. Even if you were to hire the services of others, it would be best for you to have the basic knowledge of what needs to be done. Therefore, you need to focus on learning a certain skill well so that you can earn money for offering that service. Once you identify a skill that you have a passion for or are good at, do your best to improve upon it. In every industry, the most highly paid people are the ones who offer a skill or service at which they excel over others.

The internet has made it very easy for you to access knowledge, improve your skill set, and learn high-income skills. You are not obliged to go to university or college to learn skills that are crucial in building wealth. There are many websites that can help you learn these skills at affordable prices. Some such websites include

- Udemy
- Coursera
- edX
- Codecademy
- Skillcrush
- Skillshare
- LinkedIn Learning
- Udacity

While you can learn various skills such as web designing, blockchain, digital marketing, and project management, you might also need to invest in improving soft skills like communication, teamwork, problem-solving, critical thinking, as well as time and stress management.

Lack of Education

One study that involved 400 participants showed that about 84% of the richest Americans are holders of an undergraduate qualification or a higher degree (Çam, 2017). Such statistics suggest that you have better chances of getting rich when you are more educated. Degrees are offered in colleges and universities, where your age is not a limiting factor. Therefore, you can enroll for a degree at any stage of your life.

It is also important to note that a lack of education does not completely shut you out from the opportunities to accumulate wealth. There are records of "university dropouts" who became counted among the richest people in the world. Mark Zuckerberg and Bill Gates both dropped out of Harvard University but still made billions from Facebook and Microsoft, respectively (Harrison, 2018). Other rich university dropouts that you might be familiar with are Harold Dell, Paul Allen, and Sheldon Adelson. So, the fact that you don't have a college degree does not mean you can't get rich—you still can!

Lack of Money

For you to make money, you will certainly need capital. When you don't have it, this can hinder your progress. While money is that important, the fact that you are currently poor should not completely thwart your hope of becoming rich. Have you ever heard Oprah Winfrey's story? Well, she was one of the poorest girls that ever walked the face of the earth, but today, she is one of the most known self-made billionaires in the U.S. Although the circumstances surrounding Winfrey's story are not the same as yours, you can derive motivation from the female billionaire's story.

Sometimes, all you need is to look at your lack of money from a completely different angle. Instead of viewing it as an obstacle to acquiring more wealth, you could see it as your motivation. Ralph Lauren did that and it worked to his advantage. During an interview, Lauren said about his childhood that he always had a passion for "clothes," though he had no money to make his dream come true at the time. Even when he had no choice but to wear the clothes that he got from his brothers, Lauren still felt some unique energy that was associated with the desire to "get his own things and make his own statement" (Woods, 2017). It's that same energy that later developed into something tangible— a fashion brand that is worth approximately $8 billion. When you have the right energy, you can turn the little that you have into billions once you get the chance. You can do this!

Unavailability of Spousal Support

Lack of spousal or a partner's support can be your "why not." It's easier to make it in any endeavor when you have emotional, financial, or spiritual support from the people who are closest to you, especially partners. While this can be quite derailing at first, don't give up on your main goal. You can look for support elsewhere, just so you can keep on. Friends, relatives, colleagues, and parents can stand by you and offer you the support that you need.

Poor Credit Scores

A credit score is a number between 300 and 850 that proves your worthiness to borrow money from creditors and lenders. When your credit score is below 670, it is regarded as low. Credit scores are based on your credit history and reflect issues such as debt, how quickly you pay back your loans, and the number of accounts you have open. If you have a higher credit score, this means creditors are more likely to lend you money because they will trust you can pay back your debt on time. This means that having a lower credit score can be an issue, because money lenders won't be able to trust you enough to give you loans. This is based on the assumption that you may not be able to make timely and full payments. If ever you do get loans, then they will be accompanied by high interest rates.

A bad credit score may also affect your employment opportunities, insurance needs, and credit card, among other things, so it is normal for you to worry about it. The better news is that bad credit scores can be fixed. You will realize that there are three main factors that affect your credit score, and fortunately, all of them can be addressed. These are

- **A short account history**: The length of time during which you have been using credit has a 15% impact on your credit score (McGurran, 2019). The shorter that period, the lower the credit score.

- **Loan balances**: The money that you currently owe covers 30% of your credit score (McGurran, 2019). Therefore, reducing this amount as much as possible will positively impact the score. Make arrangements to pay up your debts and redeem your credit score. Meanwhile, you can consider pausing the use of your cards. If you require more time to lower your debt balances, check if you can qualify for a balance transfer card. This card comes with an interest-free period during which you are "protected" from many charges as you do everything possible to clear your balances. Once you have the balance transfer card, be sure to make your payments within the period when the interest-free benefit is still valid.

- **High credit usage**: Having many credit cards may also negatively affect your credit score because you might be viewed as trying to borrow from various sources. This factor makes up 10% of your credit score (McGurran, 2019). During the time when you are increasing your credit score, pause the idea of applying for a new credit card.

- **Payment history**: Your payment history accounts for 30% of your credit score (McGurran, 2019). If you do everything possible to make your payments, including toward bills, on time, this will gradually increase your credit score. If you have payments that have similar due dates, which may make it more difficult for you to pay up, you might need to consider rescheduling the cut-off dates.

Mental Obstacles

Endeavors to make more money are noble, but they come with a lot of changes to your lifestyle. Such changes may be challenged by certain mental barriers like worry and doubt. This is mainly because, while change is inevitable, it can be accompanied by a lot of uncertainty. As you go through this section, be encouraged to face mental obstacles and overcome them. We will go through some of the common mental obstacles that may negatively affect your journey to make more money.

Worry

Making strides toward being different will certainly attract some level of opposition, and the goal to accumulate wealth is not an exception. Therefore, do not worry about what other people will say. Although the desire for approval is part of human life, don't let it ruin your well-thought-out plan to prosper. Worrying won't change your future, so flow with the moments and let your plans unfold. Activities such as meditation also come in handy when dealing with worry.

Blame

Truth be told, you will not be able to control everything that comes your way as you journey toward your money-making goal. When things get hard and uncomfortable, it is easy to point fingers at others in a bid to make ourselves feel better. Sometimes, we end up killing the zeal in the people who would positively contribute to our reaching our financial goals in the process. If you want your journey to be more seamless, do away with the "blame game." Being a player in this game will only shift your focus away from strategizing on the next effective step that you should be implementing to redirect the situation and make sure it doesn't ruin your plans. So rather pause, face your challenges, and take responsibility for the adverse situation, and success will be yours.

Fear

Do you sometimes get scared of taking the next step? Well, that's fear of risk. Could it be that you have the "what if I lose" kind of mindset? It's a common type of fear, too, especially when you are investing the little that you have to make things better for yourself. What you feel is completely normal because everyone goes through that experience at some point in their lives. However, what matters is how you handle the fear, and whether you succumb to it or you challenge it.

In the book *Rich Dad Poor Dad*, the rich dad made a statement when he said about the Texans, "They're proud when they win, and they brag when they lose. Texans have a saying, 'If you're going to go broke, go big.' You don't want to admit you went broke over a duplex. Most people around here are so afraid of losing, they don't have a duplex to go broke with" (Kiyosaki, 2012). Develop the culture of embracing failure if you truly want to be successful. Don't just focus on the "what if I fail" side of the story, but on what if you win? Your mindset should be focused on winning, though you should be ready to face failure if it ends up being the only available option at a particular time.

Poor Self-Confidence

Looking at yourself and thinking that there is no way you can ever make huge amounts of money is a true reflection of a lack of self-confidence. In the next chapter, we will further explore how best you can "believe in yourself."

Envy

While we can present more or less the same methods for getting rich, you should always know that you are different from the next person. Understanding this will help you to recognize that you are not in a competition with anyone, so you should maintain your own path. If a colleague makes money through public speaking, be happy for them and continue with what you can do best. Envy can waste a lot of time that you could have been using to get rich through a method that works for you. Work on being a master of your own trade, and stop wasting your energy on envying others.

Obstructing Thoughts

Steve Siebod did 25 years of research on millionaires. He then wrote a book called *How Rich People Think*, in which he emphasized that "It wasn't the lack of desire that held the masses back from getting wealthy, but the lack of belief in their own ability to make it happen" (Elkins, 2017). Getting rich begins in your mind before you start taking the relevant action. So, what kinds of thoughts often run through your mind? It's important to know that those thoughts might be the ones hindering you from getting rich. If you are wondering what kind of thoughts might be barriers to your financial success, here are some ideas:

- **I should be a genius if I want to become rich**: The fact that not everyone who got a Cum Laude in college is rich is a clear sign that getting rich is less about excelling in examinations. Accumulating wealth has nothing to do with being "smart."

- **If "so and so" can't be rich, then who am I to make it?**: This brings us back to the issue of the inferiority complex. You deserve to be rich just like any other person out there. So, flex up and replace such thoughts with the "I deserve to be rich" kind of mindset.

- **I need money to start making money:** Yes, your capital for making more money could be money, but there are other alternatives, too. Time, talent, and energy can be your capital to start raising money. Therefore, don't limit yourself—you can start from where you are with what you have at your disposal.

- **I can be rich, but only if I work hard**: Working hard can get you started on the journey to becoming rich, but you should learn to use leverage to accumulate wealth. It's that ability to think of solutions to the world's problems, as well as out-thinking your competitors, that will make you better.

- **Making money is difficult, let alone accumulating it**: This kind of thought makes you feel that making money is an extremely complicated endeavor. As mentioned earlier, money is made by addressing problems that communities, countries, and continents are facing. You can also grow your money by investing it. That's not necessarily complicated, is it?

- **If I can get enough money to support myself when I retire, I am good to go**: These thoughts are not a reflection of a "rich mindset" because you are limiting yourself. As a result, you will only work on accumulating money that is enough for you to survive up to your death, and that is unlikely to be lots of money. On the other hand, when you focus on impacting the world, you stretch your ability further.

- **It's not up to me to get rich**: These types of thoughts are a sure way of accepting defeat by poverty. Becoming rich is not something that is beyond your control. Rather, it is an inside job in which you are actively involved.

- **There is no way I can successfully pursue both riches and family life**: Considering the many responsibilities that women have in families, it is easier to think this way. There is no rule that says you should choose between accumulating wealth and being a family woman. You can certainly do both by customizing a balance between the two.

- **Money is the cause of all evil acts in this world**: Money also motivates good acts, like charitable activities. The actual root of evil is bad thoughts, not money.

- **No one in my family line has ever been rich**: That could be true, but there is nothing that can stop you from being the first one to get rich in your family. In fact, be determined to change history by becoming rich.

It is true that when you are forewarned, you are fore-armed. Becoming aware of the obstacles that might come your way increases the likelihood of victory when you finally come across them. Keep in mind that these obstacles are nothing more than tests of your resilience and self-confidence, and they will play a crucial role in winning. Get ready to boost your self-esteem by reading the next chapter, which delves deeper into the aspects of "believing in yourself."

Chapter 4:

Believing in Yourself

To be successful at anything, believing in yourself is the fundamental state of mind you need to adopt. As a woman, you might doubt that you can get rich due to gender-related factors like the wealth gap between males and females. It's an issue of hurt self-confidence, right? At times, it could be that you never had self-esteem for as long as you can remember, but let's face it: You will need to believe in yourself to make it financially or otherwise. The main goal of this chapter is to motivate you to believe that you are the right candidate to achieve the financial goals that you set for yourself. You will have to trust yourself in this.

Failure Is Part of the Process. Embrace It!

One of the common themes among self-made, financially successful people is that, while they are open to advice from trusted advisors, they always maintain an "I believe in myself" kind of attitude. As a result, when other people expose them to negativity or tell them a thousand reasons why they can't do something, they keep a strong belief in themselves. They understand that failure on one item or task is just a steppingstone to ultimate success. By the way, you only truly fail when you quit, and you are certainly not a quitter. Michael Jordan, who is one of the most famous basketball players of all time, once said, "I've missed more than 9,000 shots in my career. I've lost almost 300 games; 26 times, I've been trusted to take the game-winning shot and missed. I've failed over and over and over again in my life. And that is why I succeed" (Fearless Motivation, 2017). Failure is usually part of the "success package" in any area of your life, even financially, which is why you should embrace it. To give your confidence a boost, let's look at some people who failed many times but still made it in the end.

Thomas Edison

Thomas Edison is the man who invented the durable light bulb. It's something that anyone would say "Wow!" to, but did you know how many times he failed before he hit the jackpot? It is believed that Edison's count of failures reached between 3,000 and 6,000 trials. Yes, that's quite a lot, and that's why he was able to get to the solution. If he had stopped at, say, 10, 50, 100, or 1,000, he wouldn't have made such an astounding innovation that impacted the whole world.

Interestingly, Edison ventured into a field that many other people had ventured into before him but without finding the solution. The bulbs that others before him made were not yet cost-effective and durable, yet his mental resilience made him want to give it a try. You can learn something from this—that just because many other people tried to get rich and did not make it doesn't mean that you won't make it, either. Instead of getting discouraged each time you try and fail, remember that Edison probably felt like he was getting closer to the solution rather than becoming discouraged. This is reflected in his words when he said, "Results! Why, man, I have gotten lots of results! I know several thousand things that won't work!" (Edison, n.d.). In essence, knowing what won't work is a step toward what possibly works.

J. K. Rowling

Maybe you want to read about a fellow female who failed before making it to success—J. K. Rowling is one such woman! Rowling is the author of *Harry Potter* and tried to publish her book, but it was rejected 12 times. At that time, she was not even close to being counted among the rich. She was just a single mom whose survival was hinged on welfare. It was only on the 13th attempt that *Harry Potter* went through, and the book became one of the major hits of all time, popular with young and old alike. The book was even translated into a movie, which was a booming success. This breakthrough made Rowling one of the richest authors of her time. Now, imagine what could have happened if Rowling had not believed in herself and had hidden the book somewhere in her old cupboards with the justification that four or ten publishers had rejected it. She certainly wouldn't be where she is today.

Oprah Winfrey

You could think of Oprah Winfrey's life as that of a sad story with a happy ending, and that is because she didn't quit, even after the many setbacks that she had to go through. Winfrey's background was characterized by poverty, and she, unfortunately, became a victim of rape at the young age of nine. This was an age during which she needed parental love and encouragement to make it in life, and she didn't quite get either of the two. This partly relates to what we are saying in this chapter—don't wait for people to encourage you because they might not. Believe in yourself instead. When she grew up, Winfrey got a TV job, and early in her career, she was fired. Not only that, but after getting another job, she also experienced a demotion from hosting evening news. Even at that, it is impressive to know that Winfrey then became an owner of a production company and hosted the best-ever American talk show. She is now a self-made billionaire despite a history of failures. Whatever the setbacks, continue to believe in yourself, and know that you are actually writing a success story.

Vera Wang

Sometimes, failure is there to redirect your path so that you can hit the right buttons for success. The story of Vera Wang is a good example of this scenario. Wang started off as a figure skater, but she couldn't be part of the U.S. Olympic Figure Skating Team in 1968. This was one mark of failure that made her quit skating, but she did not give up on life. Wang took up a job as an assistant at *Vogue* three years later when she was 22 years old. It took her only one year to assume a new and better role as a senior fashion editor in the same company. She was then promoted to an editor-in-chief position after 23 years of hard work in her previous position.

Little did Wang know that all these steps up were part of her route to becoming an incredible fashion designer. Mind you, all this wouldn't have been possible if she had pursued a career in figure skating, where she probably wouldn't have made it that big. Therefore, we can learn from Wang's story that failure can be one of the major steps toward your actual success. This doesn't necessarily mean that failure should feel pleasant. You will certainly feel disappointment, frustration, and any other negative feelings that are associated with the result, but what you do afterward is what determines whether you will be successful or not. Ideally, you will need to accept that things didn't go your way but then you should rise and dust yourself off; tell yourself "I can do it!" and soldier on like a warrior.

Ariana Huffington

The first book that Ariana Huffington authored was received without much resistance, but this was not the case with her second one. The second book was subject to rejection by 36 publishers, and that was probably enough to make her give up on it. The fact that she maintained her optimism and continued to believe in herself is what made her live to witness her success. You certainly need the same attitude and resilience to conquer the "why nots" that might be waiting for you on your way to becoming the rich woman that you wish to be.

James Dyson

If you use a vacuum cleaner often, have you ever wondered how long it took for "the Dyson" to be invented? James Dyson spent a whopping 15 years trying to come up with a vacuum cleaner. He even made 5,126 different versions before investing in the one that finally worked. Dyson made a fortune when his vacuum cleaner finally hit stores in 1993, but that was after 15 years of patience and perseverance.

How to Believe in Yourself to Conquer the "Why Nots"

How many times have you tried to become rich? Could it be five, ten, twenty, or fifty times? Whatever the number, I would like to congratulate you for going through the process. Those "failures" are part of the number of steps that you need before you can achieve your ultimate goal, so they were never a waste of time. In one interview, Thomas Edison was asked how it felt for him to fail 1,000 times in a bid to develop the incandescent light bulb. His response was, "I didn't fail 1,000 times. The light bulb was an invention with 1,000 steps." So, you never know how many steps you need to reach your financial goal, but be patient and walk the journey. Besides patience, what other attributes do you need to develop to be resilient enough to move on after a series of failures? We will answer this question in this section as we look at some of the characteristics that we can learn from people like Edison, Winfrey, Wang, and Rowling.

Define a Better Relationship Between Your Past and Future

Some things that you went through in your life were not avoidable, so there is no need for you to blame yourself for them. You were probably a victim of circumstances, but that does not mean that your future will be like that, too. In other words, don't let bad things that already happened shape your future in a bad way. For example, if you tried to make $10,000 before and it didn't work, that is not a sure sign that you cannot be a millionaire. Find something from your previous experience and use it as encouragement. Like in the previous example, you could probably identify what went wrong and use that as your motivation to develop that "I am well able" kind of push.

See the Broader Picture

Even if there are two or three things in your life that didn't work, there are some that you excelled in, right? Don't let what didn't work override the ones that did to the extent that you don't recognize the latter anymore. If you focus on what could not work, this is what will brew the inferiority complex in you, and you will be less likely to become confident enough to tackle bigger goals in life. Therefore, no matter what, remember the good moments and achievements, because these are sure signs that you have the ability to succeed.

Set Up Clear Goals

Just waking up and living an unplanned life can make winning more difficult, and this may negatively impact your self-confidence. It's like going to war unprepared. Remember that all goals have challenges that you will meet along the way, and the way you deal with these obstacles might be better when you have planned your steps well. Going back to the war comparison, you are less likely to be ambushed, and even if you are, you still have a good chance of coming out of it alive. So, setting your goals can boost your confidence in tackling them, and you might even achieve them faster. Imagine walking up to a place that you have never been to without GPS or any idea of where you are going. You will get tired before you start the journey; that is, if you even embark on it in the first place. The situation is different when you know where you are going. With GPS, you can picture the journey and your destination even though you have not been there before. Simply put, your confidence, when you have a good GPS device, is more or less the same as that of someone who has been to that place physically. Well-set goals are like GPS toward the financial state that you want to achieve.

Own and Control Your Emotions

No doubt you go through a wide range of feelings, both good and bad depending on the circumstances. Even as you journey toward your financial and other goals, you will still experience different emotions. However, how you react to them can build or harm your self-esteem. Train yourself to be emotionally stable. One of the strategies that might work for you is allowing yourself to calm down before you make decisions on how to act. You are more likely to make a positive move this way, and that will boost or maintain the belief that you have in yourself.

Monitor Your Body Language

You might be wondering what body language has to do with the confidence that you need to make money, right? Well, that's a good question. If believing in yourself is your main goal at the moment, then there are objectives that feed into that goal. This means that those seemingly little things that you do to boost your self-confidence will contribute to the bigger picture of the confident version of yourself. In a similar way, hanging your head, slouching, and shallow breathing are a reflection of the negative states that you might be in, and this body language has nothing to do with being confident. Your posture, eye contact, and breathing pattern should show that you believe in yourself. This is something that you can train yourself to maintain over time as you build your self-confidence.

Practice Self-Love

We all tend to put our confidence in the people we love, right? So, to be confident with yourself, you also need to make yourself your "first love." Don't confuse this with being selfish, it's as simple as it sounds—give love to yourself. Once you are able to love yourself for who you are, you will be able to build your self-esteem. You will begin to respect and guard your values, strengths, weaknesses, and everything else that defines you. That is the main root of believing in yourself.

Work on Your Self-Talk

What do you say about yourself? Who do you say you are? Your self-talk contributes much to your confidence, which is why you need to learn to direct positive things toward yourself. You can actually live your dream in your mind before it manifests physically, and this is revealed through your positive talk and affirmations. The more you speak positively about and toward yourself, the more you feel confident. You will come across times when your negativity seems to be making decisions for you, and you have no option but to run with it. Even at that, train yourself to speak positive things, though it might feel absurd. Look yourself in the mirror and tell yourself

- I can do this.
- I am ready to make my first million.

- I have what it takes to reach my financial goal.

- Obstacles along the way make me better, stronger, and bigger, and I am ready for the experience.

- Good morning, lady. Are you ready for another winning expedition?

Deal With Limiting Beliefs

There are some beliefs that have stuck around long enough for them to be regarded as actually true to the extent that they limit your thoughts and abilities. These are what we are referring to as limiting beliefs. For example, if no one in your family line ever became a millionaire, you might limit yourself to a certain range of income. This is the kind of limiting belief that you need to break while you develop a new growth mindset.

Remember Your Accomplishments

Take some time to look at the things that you were able to accomplish in the past. Such things are a solid reminder that you are capable of doing great things. Do you have any medals that you won? If you have any certificates or any other evidence that you once made it, embrace them and tell yourself, "I can do this! I have done other things well in the past, after all!"

Shift Your Focus

At times, all it takes for you to start believing in yourself is shifting your focus toward the things that motivate you. Just as there are always two sides to every coin, so it is with different situations in life. There are positive and negative sides, depending on how you see them. Your self-esteem is drained when you focus on the negativity that is associated with situations. Train your mind to identify the positive things and embrace them. Let's assume that you do a PowerPoint presentation and during the question time, people in the audience ask you too many questions compared to the previous presenters. You might think that people have so many questions because you did not present well, but what if it's just because people found your presentation so interesting that they became curious to know more? Always shift your focus to more positivity.

Mind Your Company

What kind of people do you spend most of your time with? The more you spend time with people who have a negative mindset, the greater the likelihood that you might follow suit. Surround yourself with people who are determined to achieve challenging goals. You need colleagues who can see the good in you and encourage you to bring out the best version of yourself—people who can help you to believe in yourself.

Activity

The activity that we will do as we end this chapter is based on creating SMART goals (Boogaard, 2021). SMART is an acronym for

- **Specific**: You should pinpoint what you want to achieve.

- **Measurable**: There should be some parameters that you use to assess your progress toward achieving your goal.

- **Achievable**: Is the goal something that is within the limits of things that can be done? There is no point in setting a goal to fly just like the birds do. You will spend a lifetime trying to achieve that, yet you never will.

- **Realistic**: How much money do you want to raise in a year? Does that amount match with the possible available resources, among other factors? Be realistic so that you don't get discouraged along the way.

- **Time-bound**: The progress of goal achievement cannot be measured unless there are time frames involved.

In one study, about 76% of the people who noted down their goals and presented progress reports to friends were able to achieve their goals (Chi, 2022). Only 33% of the participants did not write their goals down but still achieved them. Based on this information, the likelihood of achieving your goals increases when you write them down and consistently follow up.

The Key Action

In Chapter 2, we created a "why" card. Now you are going to make a "goal" card on the back of the one that has your "why." The idea of the goal card is the brainchild of Napoleon Hill as he presented it in his book "*Think and Grow Rich*" (Taleb, 2018). Please write out this goal as if you have already achieved it, not as if you are still looking forward to it. For example, here is what you could write on your "goal card":

"I'm so happy and grateful now that I have no debt and have accumulated $25,000 in the past year, and am well on my way to my first million."

Now you have an index card that has your "why(s)" on one side and your intermediate-term goal on the other side. You should be looking at this card every day, and by doing so, your subconscious mind will begin to believe this. If you keep telling yourself something often enough, you will start to believe it. The "why" and "goal" cards are meant to help motivate you while enhancing the belief that you have in yourself at the same time.

The main aim of this chapter was to motivate you to believe in yourself because you are the main resource that you have to realize your goals. Hopefully, it has improved the way you see yourself and your goals. Such a scenario allows us to transition well to the next chapter, where we will start to delve deeper into the nitty-gritty of making money, starting with laying the right foundation of good personal finance.

Chapter 5:

Before You Build, You Must

Lay the Foundation

In the previous chapters, our main focus was to prepare you and help you develop a mindset that is required in the art of making money. This chapter marks the transition to the nitty-gritty of *actually* accumulating financial wealth. For any building to stand, it will require a strong foundation. If you don't put the proper foundation in place, your future efforts will ultimately collapse. So, what is this foundation I'm referring to? We are talking about the fundamental, foundational principles of *personal finance* that you should put in place first before you move on to the next steps of actually "getting rich." If you don't put these fundamentals in place, then the later steps that we will describe in subsequent chapters are more likely to fail.

Never Underestimate the Importance of a Strong Foundation

As we highlighted earlier on, even the most beautiful buildings collapse when the foundation is poor. In a similar manner, no matter the financial growth that you might seem to be enjoying, if the foundation of basic financial management is not there, success might be short-lived. Here are a couple examples of buildings that collapsed due to foundation failure (Foundation Repair, 2020):

- **The Ocean Tower**: The Ocean Tower was built in Texas and was supposed to be a 31-story building. However, foundation issues caused it to begin sinking and leaning, which is why it was then demolished before completion.

- **The Transcona grain elevator**: This was a facility for storing grain and was used by the Canadian Pacific Railways. When the grain was loaded into the storage facility in 1913, the building began to slowly sink. The grain elevator then sank about one foot into the ground within an hour after the grain was removed. It then tilted 27 degrees toward the west in less than a day.

You don't want any of these examples to be a reflection of what could happen to your finances, right? The solution is easy— create strong financial basics by understanding and implementing the fundamentals of money as discussed in the next section.

The Basics of Personal Finance

Finance is a field that deals with the management of money. There are three main types of finance, and these are personal, corporate, and public. For the purposes of this chapter, we will focus on the first one. There are many aspects that are involved in personal finance, and these include budgeting, investing, saving, lending, borrowing, and forecasting. Unless you master the financial basics that we will discuss in this section, managing and growing your money could be a challenge. So, as you learn the finance fundamentals, be sure to make necessary adjustments to the way you are currently handling your money-related issues. This will help you to prepare yourself for the implementation of what you will learn in later chapters.

The Fundamentals of Budgeting

Budgeting is a financial management tool that helps you to allocate your money for various purposes before taking any action of spending it. In other words, a budget gives you a forecast of how you will spend your money and how much you will save. Budgeting assists you to live within your means and avoid getting into debt, especially if you strictly follow it. With a good budget, you can determine things that you need to prioritize as you spend your money. Simply put, budgeting is a great tool for avoiding the mismanagement of funds that might derail you from getting rich. Even if you are to get rich, you will still need to create a budget so that you can avoid random and avoidable impulse spending. In this section, we will highlight major steps that you cannot do without when you are setting up a budget.

Determine Your Monthly Income

The first thing that you need to do is to determine the amount of money that you have at your disposal. To do this, write down all your sources of income, including your salary, business profits, as well as child support and social security funds. Write down the income that you expect from each of these sources in a month's time. Please be sure to use the amount that you get after all taxes have been removed because this is the actual amount that you will receive. Add the values to come up with the total amount of expected income.

Determine Your Expenses

When you create your budget, you should separate your expenses into fixed and variable ones. Fixed expenses are those that remain stable over a long time. For example, rentals may remain the same for, say, a year before they change, so they are categorized as a fixed expense. Mortgage and car payments are also fixed expenses. Variable expenses tend to change and are relatively unpredictable, so you can only estimate them. Good examples include groceries and medical expenses. List down your expenses and write down the amount of money that you will spend on each item.

Among the fixed and variable expenses that you list, you will be surprised to note that some of them are mandatory while others are discretionary. For instance, rent, food, childcare, water, electricity, health insurance, and medical prescriptions are some of the mandatory expenses that you certainly can't do without. On the other hand, you could do without eating out, buying new clothes, leisure travel, and fitness memberships. Now, follow through with your lists of expenses and add a "star" or "tick" against all the discretionary expenses. Doing this will help you to set your priorities right, especially when your budget is tight. So, in the case that your income is too low for the listed expenses, you can take out discretionary ones.

Income Minus the Expenses

Now, it's time to subtract the total expenses from the income that you are projecting. It will be good if there is a significant amount left after performing this process. This means that you have excess money left after covering your expenses, and this could be the amount that you can channel toward savings. However, if your balance becomes negative, then you certainly need to revisit your list of expenses and take out discretionary expenses until you get a positive balance. You might also want to review some of the mandatory expenses to see if their financial allocations can be reduced. For example, you could cut down on your list of food items or go for a cheaper health insurance plan.

Forecast Your Budget

You can use the budget that you have created as a template that you can use for, say, a year to come. You could be making slight adjustments where necessary to match the specifications for each month.

Dealing With Debt

While loans might seem to help you cover some expenses, they might get out of hand. You don't want to get to such a state because then you can't make any progress toward your "get rich" goal. It is difficult, if not impossible, for you to save when you are in deep debt. It is true that there are many circumstances that might cause you to get into debt, and these include life's emergencies and unorganized spending. Whatever the source, debts can be gradually reduced and ultimately eliminated. If you are wondering how this can be achieved, go through the following debt reduction strategies:

- **Stop taking more loans**: Avoid the urge to borrow more, as this will only take you deeper into debt. It is better to maintain the debt at the level where it is while you make arrangements to reduce it.

- **Create and assess your budget**: Use the steps that we described in the previous section to create a budget and then evaluate it to see where you can cut down on your expenses. This will leave you with more money to channel toward paying down your debt.

- **Pay beyond the minimum**: Paying the minimum amount for your debt installments is good, but paying more is better. Making bigger payments will assist you to clear the debt at a faster rate while you also avoid higher interest rates. Simply put, the shorter the period during which you pay on the debt, the lower the total interest. All you have to do is add an extra amount to the minimum payable amount.

- **Sell things that you don't need**: The whole idea behind selling some of the things that you have is to create more income that you can use to pay off your debt.

- **Refinance the debt**: Refinancing your debt is another strategy for reducing the total interest involved. One of the ways through which you can do this is by getting a personal loan whose interest rates are much lower than your current debts. So, you cover the debts and remain with the loan that has a lower interest rate. The "transfer" option requires you to do thorough research so that you can determine the best options with the best rates. If you are dealing with credit card debt, transferring the debt to a balance transfer card also works well. With balance transfer cards, you won't need to pay interest for a stipulated period of time, which is sometimes up to 18 months. This option is only possible if you are sure that you will be able to make the payments within the interest-free time frame.

- **Use the debt snowball strategy**: Let's say you have five different debts that you are paying off. Based on the debt snowball method, you can pay the minimum payable amounts for the four bigger debts, and then pay as much as possible for the smallest one. As a result, you will quickly clear the smallest debt while reducing the principal amounts for the bigger ones. You continue with the strategy on the four remaining ones, to the effect that you also clear the second smallest debt. Before you know it, you will have cleared all your debts.

- **Windfalls can help**: Windfalls, whether expected or unexpected, can be channeled into paying off your debts. These include work bonuses, inheritances, tax refunds, or even cash gifts. Instead of using all the money from windfalls for fun and other things, allocating some or all of it to debt payments may assist you to pay off debt much faster.

- **Increase streams of income**: Paying your debt can be a challenge if you are looking at one source of income, especially if it's not even enough to sustain yourself. Coming up with other ideas for making money can help to loosen things a bit. For instance, if you have a talent or passion that can earn you some extra dollars, it's worth giving it a try. This could be writing, art, acting, or even buying and selling.

An Emergency Fund

Keeping aside some extra money in case of emergencies is one of the main basics of good personal finance management. Ideally, it is recommended that you accumulate funds that can cover at least three months of your current living expenses. This not only gives you peace of mind when things go wrong, but it also keeps you out of debt. However, statistics also show that the emergency savings of approximately 51% of people cannot take them through three months of their living expenses (Bennett, 2022). An emergency fund also comes in handy in the event of unplanned expenses like car and house repairs, as well as medical bills. Sometimes, starting an emergency fund can seem so difficult, or even impossible, but once you try it, you will realize that it is worth the effort. We will make things easier for you by highlighting how you can start creating your emergency fund.

- **Tweak your budget**: You should have some extra funds for you to be able to create an emergency fund; otherwise, you will end up taking from the saved money again. This means that you have to play around with your budget to see where you can reduce your expenses. Do not cut down too much on the mandatory expenses, rather reduce the discretionary ones.

- **Come up with emergency fund goals**: As you start off, it is better to create several savings goals that are relatively smaller. Beginning with one bigger goal for, say, five months, could easily discourage you. How about starting with a two-week goal, or even a month's stretch is better. Since the probability of achieving small goals is higher, this will encourage you to try bigger goals. This way, you gradually master the art of saving without straining yourself beyond your ability.

- **Begin by saving smaller amounts**: If you strain your finances too much as you try to save more, you increase the chances of giving up along the way. Remember, the journey of a thousand miles begins with one step. Start with smaller amounts, be it $20, $50, or $100. However, be sure to make these deposits at regular intervals so that you are consistently adding something to your emergency fund.

- **Set up automated, direct deposits**: Try to avoid the scenario where you have to touch the money before transferring it to an emergency fund account. Automated deposits are better because you cannot use excuses such as forgetting. So, once your paycheck comes in, the savings amount is directed to the account that you designated for emergency funds. It's also possible to use savings apps that direct a certain percentage of your paycheck directly to your savings account.

- **Set a limit for your emergency fund**: As much as the emergency fund is vital, you don't want to save unlimitedly in this account. Once you reach your ultimate goal, consider channeling your savings to another account that allows your money to earn more interest. For example, you can use a retirement account and your money will grow over time. The interest rates for savings accounts are quite low because the money that you put there is easily accessible.

Doing Away With Credit Cards

Reports from the Federal Reserve show that about 80% of all Americans who are adults own at least one credit card (Martin, 2019). These are sad statistics, considering the negative effects that are associated with these plastic cards. Doing away with credit cards is one of the ways through which you can learn to live within your means. You might be surprised to notice that the money that you earn is actually enough to cater to all your needs and some of your wants, depending on how you set up your budget. Using credit only promotes more uncontrolled spending, and the stress that comes with paying off the debts can be an awful experience. So, the important question becomes, "What can I do to live without credit cards?" Fortunately, there is a lot that you can do. Take a look at the following nuggets:

- **Stick to your budget**: Of course, this is the number one rule! Create a good budget that matches your income and train yourself never to stray from it.

- **Plan for major activities and events:** Have you ever been in situations where a family friend suggests a trip or an outing and you quickly jump into accepting the idea without thinking much about how you will fund the venture? When such things happen, the next thing you think about is a credit card. Avoiding this trap is easy— plan for all events so you won't have to depend on credit cards to make things happen. Again, remain within the boundaries of what you can afford.

- **Get the cards out of your wallet**: Moving around with a credit card is enough temptation because you might end up using it. Take it out of your wallet and make a solid decision never to use it again. You can still use your debit card or even cash for making necessary payments.

Living Within Your Means

We have already touched on some of the things that can help you to live within your means. These include budgeting, clearing debts, having an emergency fund, and getting rid of credit cards. You can also come up with strategies that simplify your financial affairs so that they are easier to manage. I will give you an example of what I do. I set up auto payments for my regular monthly expenses to ensure that my bills are always paid on time. To this effect, I use three bank accounts as follows:

- **A bill payment account**: This is where our regular monthly bills, like utilities and insurance, are automatically withdrawn. Then, each month I top this account up to a pre-set amount that I know is more than enough to cover all our automatic bills.

- **A spending account**: This is the one that my spouse and I get our discretionary money from each month. We can use this money to buy gas, groceries, gifts, and for dining out. Again, we top-up this account each month to a set dollar value, and then that is all the money we have to spend for the month. It is possible to do this on a weekly or biweekly basis, depending on your preference.

- **A savings account**: This is the one we use to save toward annual or long-term goals, such as putting together funds for Christmas, buying a car, or going on a vacation. We then "pay cash" for everything that we want to do once we've saved the money so we do not use a credit card or loan.

This chapter guided you through some aspects of creating a strong financial foundation that will propel you to reaching the $1 million dollar mark, as you desire. We recommend that you visit the resources page, start reviewing the information we've provided there, and then begin to take the steps to lay your solid financial foundation. It is from that foundation that you will then be able to build on as you go through the remaining chapters of this book, which describe the three methods that you can use to reach your first $1 million.

Chapter 6:

Get Rich Method 1—The

Train

One study that was done by Fidelity revealed that about 88% of all millionaires are self-made, meaning that they were not born into wealth (Sightings, 2018). Interestingly, three predominant ways of getting rich were observed among all the self-made millionaires. Here, we're defining "rich" as being a millionaire, despite the fact that there are different levels of being rich. However, from many people's viewpoint, having a net worth of $1 million plus, while not "filthy rich," is still lightyears ahead of living "paycheck to paycheck," not to mention the substantial amount of security and freedom that this financial status provides.

In this book, we've decided to describe these three main ways of getting rich as "the train, the plane, and the rocket." This nomenclature is mainly based on the speed at which the goal of becoming rich is more likely to be reached. Please note that many self-made millionaires end up using more than one of the three methods of getting rich—they'll ride the train, take the plane, and maybe even hop on a rocket in their journey to their first million. However, one thing that is common among all self-made millionaires is that they all began with just *one* of the methods. Therefore, the information that we will provide in this chapter, as well as in chapters 7 and 8, will help you to make your decision with regard to which "get-rich" method you should start with. Your choice will depend on a number of factors, which include the stage at which you are in life, as well as your unique situation, skills, and preferences.

The "Train": An Overview

To kickstart your comparisons, this chapter will dwell on the "train" method. The "train" method of getting rich is slow, steady, and extremely dependable. It is based on simple math and the power of time and compounding money. You may think of the "train" strategy as simple saving and investing. Tom Corley embarked on a five-year study during which he studied the money-related habits of 225 millionaires (Corley, 2022). From the study's findings, Corley reported that approximately 88% of the millionaires that he interviewed highlighted the fact that saving was one of the fundamentals that contributed to their ability to accumulate wealth.

In yet another study, the results showed that among every four millionaires, three of them acknowledged that investing was the rollercoaster to their financial success, especially when it's done regularly, consistently, and over a relatively long time (Chang, 2022). This shows that saving and investing, a.k.a. the "train," is a relatively slow but sure method of propelling yourself toward your first million. Therefore, once you have your "personal finance foundation" in order, you can then start building on it by saving and investing your way to your first million.

The fact that the "train" method may be slower than the other strategies for getting rich is, to some extent, neutralized by the advantages that are associated with it. Here are some of them:

- There are no special skills required.

- No specific level of education is needed.

- You don't need credit or money to begin.

- It is less time-consuming, so it is less likely to affect your schedule.

- The method is extremely dependable.

How Does the "Train" Work?

You might be wondering how such a slow method can ultimately make you rich. As we mentioned earlier, this method leverages the power of time, consistency, and compounding. We will further explain how this works using a few examples. Please note that in all the examples, we will use the rate of return of what the S&P 500 actually delivered over the past 50 years (1972 to 2021), which is 9.4% per year (Hall, 2021).

Example 1: Jenny's Story

Let's look at the example of Jenny, who is aged 25. Jenny has recently completed her education and is working full-time while paying her bills. Jenny has a good personal financial foundation in place, so she starts saving toward her first million.

If Jenny saved just $190 per month and got returns that are similar to the S&P 500, which are 9.4% per year, she will have accumulated $1 million in just under 40 years. This means that by the time Jenny reaches the age of 65, she will have become a millionaire, before we even include any home or other assets that she might own. So, with consistency, Jenny takes advantage of the power of time and compounding without having to save too much money in any given month.

Example 2: Sally's Story

Sally is 35 years old and also wants to "take the train" to a million dollars. Please note that we are using the same S&P 500 9.4% rate of return from the past 50 years. So, by saving $500 per month, Sally can reach the same $1 million savings goal in 30 years, by the time she is 65.

Here is an important point to note—when you save for the long term (retirement) using this method, an added benefit is that, as you accumulate funds along the way, you have access to additional financial security and "emergency funds" should you ever need it. While one would want to use their retirement savings as a "last resort," it does provide that additional benefit.

Example 3: Audrey's Story

Let's also consider Audrey, who is 45 years old. How much will she need to save per month to reach her $1 million goal? Audrey could save $1,450 per month starting at age 45. By the time she reaches the age of 65—that is, in 20 years—Audrey will have accumulated $1 million based on a 9.4% rate of return.

So, in summary, at a 9.4% annual rate of return:

- You need $190 per month to reach $1 million in 40 years.
- You need $500 per month to hit the $1 million mark in 30 years.
- You need $1,450 per month to accumulate $1 million in 20 years.

While none of the examples that we presented offer a "get rich quick" strategy, they show that saving and investing are all potentially doable without having to pump out a huge amount of extra cash each month. Moreover, they show that the "train" method is well within the reach of most women once they have their "financial house" in order, and that includes you. Again, going back to those fundamentals of personal financial management—you need to get your expenses in line with your income so that you live within your means and give yourself the ability to hop on the train and start saving each month.

Saving Versus Investing

Now that we have highlighted that both saving and investing are the pillars of the "train" method of getting rich, you might be wondering whether you should focus on one of the two or both. Well, this question is easily answered when we explore the differences between saving and investing. Moreover, some use these two terms interchangeably, but are they really the same? As you read on, you will realize that they are different even though they can complement each other. This section will help you to learn the basic concepts that are associated with saving and investing.

The Differences

The main difference between saving and investing is that the former is short-term while the latter is long-term. Saving also yields lower returns compared to investing, though the latter comes with higher risks. This means that losing your money is more probable when you invest your money than when you save it. The table below is a summary of the differences between investing and saving.

Table 1: The major differences between saving and investing (Royal, 2023)

Compared factor	Investing	Saving
Level of difficulty	More difficult	Easier
Type of account used	Brokerage	Bank
Protection in the event of inflation	More protection, especially over longer periods	Limited protection
Level of returns	Could be lower or higher, depending on the amount of money invested	Generally lower

Time frame	Usually not less than five years	Relatively short
Risk involved	Relatively higher and tends to increase when you are working with larger investments	None when the account is FDIC-insured

The Similarities

Saving and investing also share some similarities, especially in regard to the associated goals. Both are methods that help you to gradually grow your money without having to go way out of your normal budget. However, you might need to make changes in the way you spend your income so that you create room for saving and/or investing. Both saving and investing involve opening some accounts that are specialized for these purposes in financial institutions. For example, you would normally want to approach a bank to open a savings account. In the case of investing, some banks do have a brokerage arm that you can take advantage of; otherwise, you can directly approach an independent broker.

Main Principles of Saving and Investing

Saving is the art of setting aside a certain amount of your money for future use, which could be a predetermined goal or an emergency. You can access this money whenever you feel like it. However, saved money can be affected by inflation, though you can save it for this risk if you decide to invest it. As we suggested earlier in this book, you could save your money up to a certain amount for the sake of security in the case of emergencies, and then invest the rest. It is important to note that there are no "one-size-fits-all" methods for saving and investing because every situation is different. However, there are some basic principles that can assist you in determining what's best for you. We will go through these principles in this section.

Know Your Goal

Saving without any goal is non-directional, in addition to not being motivating. You want to know what you are saving your money for. In other words, what do you want to do with the money that you are putting aside? Could it be that you want to build a new house or buy a car? Are you saving toward your emergency fund? Whatever the reason might be, your goals for saving your money should be clear. While you might have other objectives along the way, your main goal, in this case, could be to accumulate your first $1 million.

Saving Should Be a Regular Activity

It is not a good idea to save only when you feel like it. Instead, it should become a habit. The advantage of saving on a regular basis is that you avoid the pressure that is associated with saving when you are faced with something that immediately requires money. Abrupt saving, compared to regular saving, can exert pressure on your daily consumption. Saving regularly is a great way of accumulating financial wealth.

Have a Target

Saving toward a preset amount usually comes with a lot of motivation. For example, now you have a goal to get hold of your first $1 million, and that alone maintains the eagerness to realize your goal. So, your target is determined by what you intend to achieve. It is also influenced by the time frame during which you want to achieve the goal. So, in your "$1 million target" case, you also need to know how much time you are giving yourself to reach it. This will also help you to come up with the minimum possible amount that you should save, say, per month.

Come Up With an Investment Horizon

An investment horizon defines the period during which the funds that you invest are unavailable for use. Again, defining this time frame helps you know how much money you will allocate for investments. Usually, longer horizons give you the leverage to widen your investments, thereby reducing the impact of the risk involved at any given moment. This is because, when the horizon is longer, this tends to spread the risk, thereby making it more reasonable and manageable.

The Earlier, the Better

The best time to start saving is now. The earlier you start, the more you make time your ally. Do you remember the examples that we discussed earlier in this chapter? Even though Jenny is just saving $190 per month starting from the age of 25, she will get the same results as Audrey, who will save $1,450 per month from the time she is 45 years old. Both ladies will reach $1 million by the time they reach 65 years of age. This is not to say that only those who are in their 20s can benefit from making time their ally. No matter your age, start from where you are and take advantage of the time factor, too.

Take Advantage of Diversification

When you invest your money, you might buy financial assets such as bonds and stocks. All financial assets carry different risk levels. However, by investing in one type of financial asset, the risk is higher, because if things do not go well with that particular asset, you might lose your money. This is where diversification comes in. When you invest in different financial assets, you spread the overall risk involved. If one investment is negatively affected in the financial market, you will still be on the safe side because the others may not be affected.

Determine the Risks That You Can Shoulder

The risks that are involved in investing require that you prepare yourself. It is not recommended that you make an investment whose risks you are not willing to shoulder, which is why it is important for you to make an assessment to determine the degree of risk that you can tolerate. This does not only involve evaluating your financial stability but also your emotional capacity as well.

Research Available Investment Options

There are many options that are available when it comes to investing. To know your best possible options, you will need to embark on some research so that you can find what suits your specific needs. If you have friends and family who have also invested before, you can ask them to share their experiences. The internet and finance books may also come in handy.

If you decide to work with a financial advisor, be sure to play an active role in deciding on the saving and investment solutions that will suit you best. When you schedule a meeting with the financial advisor, prepare for it. Be ready to ask questions, especially with regard to regulatory issues. This will help you to remain on the good side of the law as you accumulate your money.

Revisit Your Investment Solution Over Time

Remember, you select your investment solution based on factors that relate to your situation. Some of these factors may change even after you have invested. In that case, it is vital for you to regularly review your decision so that you match the current situation.

The Basic Concepts of Investing

Regardless of the investment option that you might have, the concepts that govern investing are more or less the same. Let's have a quick rundown of these concepts to enhance your basic understanding of what investing entails.

- **Risk and return**: These two correlate with each other. This means that the higher the returns, the higher the risk involved. Always bear this in mind as you make your choices among investment options so that you work with what matches your needs and risk tolerance levels.

- **Diversification of the risk**: You cannot run away from having to deal with risks as long as you are investing. The best you can do is to minimize the probability of bigger losses through the risk diversification strategy.

- **Dollar-cost averaging**: With this long-term strategy, you make fixed and regular investments as time progresses. The advantage of this strategy evens out the negative effects of short-term fluctuations in the market.

- **Compound interest**: The money that you originally pay in when you invest is called the principal. As time progresses, the principal grows because it earns interest. If you invest for longer periods of time, the interest that is earned on the principal also accumulates its own interest. This is the concept of compound interest—it has a snowball effect.

If the "train" method is the one that you would like to get started with, you can go to the resources page and select the ones that appeal to you so that you can get started with implementing this as part of your plan. We'll also be helping you to evaluate whether this method of getting rich is the best of the three methods for you to start with, based on your personal situation. Be on the lookout for this evaluation in Chapter 9 but for now, get ready to learn about the "plane" method.

Chapter 7:

Get Rich Method 2—The

Plane

The "plane method" of getting rich uses financial leverage, which is basically making money using other people's money. This is a relatively faster method of becoming a millionaire compared to the "train" that we described in the previous chapter. Upon learning about this method for the first time, a lot of people are hesitant about going through with it. However, after going through this chapter, you will be equipped with enough knowledge to know how efficient this method is and how you might make it work for you.

The Concept of Leverage

Leverage occurs when you borrow money so that you can invest in something that will give you greater returns. In simple terms, it is to use the money to gain more money. Leverage increases your reach in the financial world. We can compare financial leverage to the concept of a lever. A lever is a machine that is used to push or lift objects with less effort. With a lever, you are able to apply a larger force over a short distance at one end while exerting just a little force over a longer distance at the other. This means that the small force you put on one end is automatically converted into a larger force on the other.

Other People's Money (OPM) Explained

For you to begin your journey of becoming a millionaire, you need funding. Using OPM can come in handy for you if you do not have large amounts of money to invest. OPM refers to the capital that you get from banks, other people, or financial institutions in a bid to improve your own financial situation. This money comes in different forms, including from angel investors, bank loans, friends or family, venture capital investors, mergers, and crowdfunding. In other words, other people's money can be termed "leveraged funds."

Using OPM is completely different from self-funding. Ways of financing yourself include using your own savings, bonds, capital, home equity, stocks, and credit cards. For any business, project, or investment to get off the ground, it requires adequate funding, which you might not have on your own. This partly explains why you could opt for OPM.

Build Wealth Through Leverage

You have the potential to reach greater heights with OPM because it gives you the ability to make larger investments that may come with greater returns. In this chapter, we will focus on how you can grow your wealth using your own money combined with leveraged funds.

Example

Let's say you invest $1,000 of your own money and are confident that you will get an 8.4% rate of return. In this case, an 8.4% rate of return means you will get an $84 return on your investment per year. Now, let's say you have another opportunity to invest $1,000 of your own money. However, in this case, you have the chance to "leverage" $3,000 of OPM, assuming that you got a loan from a bank. This means you can now invest $4,000 instead of just $1,000. If you are still able to earn an 8.4% rate of return, it will be on the $4,000, which means you get a $336 growth on your $4,000 investment per year (8.4% multiplied by $4,000). This is an illustration of how you would have used "leverage" to make your $1,000 earn you higher investment returns.

It is important to note, however, that the loans you get from banks or financial institutes do not come without a fee. You will be charged interest on the amount that they lend to you. A better catch is when you are able to invest in something that will give you returns that are higher than the interest you will be charged; that is what we call "leverage." If you invest in something that earns you less than the interest you are being charged, we consider this a loss. To elaborate further on the relationship that exists between "interest" and "rate of return" when the concept of leverage is properly applied, let's look at another example.

In the previous example, you invested $1,000 of your own money, got another $3,000 from the bank, and ended up with a total of $4,000 to invest. At an 8.4% rate of return, your $4,000 investment grows by $336 per year. If your bank charges you an interest rate of 5% annually on the $3,000 they loaned to you, this is $150. To calculate your net growth per year, you subtract the $150 interest from the $336, which gives you $186. This further shows how the "plane" method gives you the potential to earn more money faster than the "train" method, which was only going to give you $84; in this case, you get $186 due to the power of leveraging.

Why Banks Prefer Real Estate

Leveraging is when you borrow money and use it to finance assets that will hopefully bring in higher returns over time. It enables you to multiply your buying power in the market. The "leverage" strategy has also been employed by companies to finance their operations so that the company's shareholder value increases. Banks prefer to lend money if you are going to invest in something that gives them a higher probability that they will get their money back. Real estate is one such venture.

Banks are drawn to real estate because it has shown to be one of the most steady and dependable asset classes over time. Real estate can be a reliable, dependable, and "easy-to-predict" way of investing. This is the reason why banks will invest in real estate, not only as loans for other people but also as a way of growing their own wealth. To best explain how effective real estate can be in helping you grow your wealth, we will look at real estate in more detail.

Real Estate Investments

Just like every other investment strategy, real estate also comes with its risks. Your duty is to make sure that the potential returns outweigh the risks. Real estate investment includes the buying and owning of property by paying a percentage of the total cost up front and then paying the balance over time. The catch in this strategy is in how you will utilize the property to make money. Real estate investment comes in different forms, which we are going to further explain in this section.

Property Rental

This is when you buy a property that can be rented. You will then rent out the property to tenants as a money-making strategy. This method is desirable because it often provides you with a regular income. However, it requires someone who has the patience to deal with tenants.

House Flipping

House flipping is almost like trading because it depends on your ability to buy an undervalued property, sell it within a short amount of time, and be able to make a profit from it. There is a longer process involved in house flipping. This is when you buy property, increase its value by renovating it, and then sell it at a profitable price. This type of estate investment can yield high returns, but it requires a deep understanding of the market.

Real Estate Investment Groups (REIGs)

REIGs are the way to go if you want to be hands-off. It works when a company builds property and then allows investors to buy portions of the property. Basically, this is how you join the group. The company is responsible for handling everything on the ground. This includes maintenance and even the tenants. The company is also responsible for finding and replacing tenants, meaning that even if some portions of the property are empty, you can still earn your income. REIGs allow you to make money while remaining hands-off regarding the day-to-day activities of the property. However, you need to keep a watchful eye on the managers who run everything on the ground to make sure that they are doing a professional job.

Risks of Real Estate Investments

As much as you have a lot to gain from using the "plane" method, you also have to be prepared to take the risks that come with it. As we previously mentioned, banks are often open to you using the "plane" method in real estate investments. Risks that come with real estate investments include structural, financial, general market, legislative, and location risks, among others.

Structural Risks

Structural risks have nothing to do with the structure of the property as the name implies. Investment is generally made up of two parts: the sponsor (the bank) and the borrower (you). This is the hierarchy that is used when it comes to payments. This means that the bank is given first priority when the profits come in, and if you are in serious need of money, you are disadvantaged.

General Market Risk

When it comes to the economy, there are key factors that control the market. This means that when you invest, you will not be immune to these factors. Your investment will be affected by things like a rise in interest rates, recession, and inflation.

Financial Risks

Financial risks all have to do with your ability to pay back the loan you will have borrowed from the bank. The amount of money you will have borrowed from the bank is directly proportional to your financial risk. Due to the fact that interest rates are constantly changing, it would be in your favor if your investment pays you more than the interest you are being charged by the bank. If the bank is charging you more than you are getting from your investment, it is considered a loss.

Legislative Risks

When it comes to the economy, you cannot run away from the legislation. For an effective investment, you need to be up to date on all changes that have occurred in the legislation. These include changes in taxes, registration processes, and tenant laws.

Location Risks

Location risks describe the issues that are associated with the positioning of your property. Factors like whether the area is urban or not are among the important aspects. Factors such as the crime rates, population, and type of shops or schools in the area determine the value of your property and the rate of return you are most likely to get.

Who Is the Plane Method Not Suited for?

The "plane" method of growing wealth does come with many undeniable benefits. However, it also comes with some risks that can be managed. You need to be equipped with the relevant knowledge in order to tackle these risks. The good news is that the potential rewards that come with using leverage can often outweigh the expected risks. With that in mind, there are situations where you might not be the right candidate to apply the "plane" method. This section of the chapter will educate you on situations that might make you ineligible to go ahead with the "plane" method of raising your net worth.

- **Unavailability of funds to top up the bank loan:** When getting a loan from the bank, you should not expect to get exactly 100% of the amount you need to buy the property you want. Banks usually provide 65% to 80% of the total amount. If you do not have the remaining 20% to 35%, you will not be able to make the investment you want to make. This means that before considering the "plane" method of growing wealth, you should save up some money on your own. For instance, if you want to buy a property that costs $500,000, the bank will likely require you to pay at least 20% of the amount, which is $100,000, and then the bank loans you the remaining $400,000. Some people opt for options like angel investors, joint ventures, crowdfunding, or getting money from family and friends if they do not have the down payment (20% to 35% of the total amount) that the bank requires from them. These options, however, are best if you are adequately knowledgeable and well-experienced in patterns that occur in the market.

- **Poor credit history**: When you are in the process of getting a loan from the bank, there are things that the bank will want to know about you. They will want to make sure that they are going to get their money back, so they will check the property they are investing in to ensure that it is in good shape and worth the risk. Most importantly, banks want to make sure that they are dealing with a dependable and trustworthy person, so they will definitely run a background check on you. A bank will run a background search of your credit history because the last thing they want is to work with someone with a bad credit score. This means that the bank will reject your loan application if you have a poor credit history. The bank will use things like your phone bills, home mortgages, car loans, and credit cards. However, this does not mean that if you have a poor or no credit history, you are completely disqualified from applying for a loan. You can use the fundamentals found in our chapter on laying a foundation to establish your financial house and rebuild your credit so that you are in a position to go to the bank and use their credit to buy your property.

- **Time constraints**: The "plane" method of building wealth requires that you invest some of your time into it. The "plane" method is completely different from the "train" method, where you just invest, sit back, and watch things unfold on their own. While real estate is considered passive, you still need some direct involvement at some point. You are the one who will be responsible for maintaining the property, as well as finding, replacing, and managing tenants. While managing a property does not typically require a full-time commitment, it will require some of your time, and if you are so busy that you cannot spare that little time, real estate investment might not be the best option for you.

The Bottom Line

Using leverage and other people's money can do wonders for your journey toward growing your wealth. You have the chance of accelerated growth and higher returns. As many ordinary real estate investors have learned in the past, real estate investment can be totally worth it, despite the risks involved. For you to become successful, you need to be willing to take on the good and the bad. You should also use strategies that decrease your chances of failure.

You need to remain focused after receiving funds and meet your aims and objectives within the time frame you initially planned. Ensure that you are getting the right kind of money from the right kind of people if you got money from a family member, friend, or investor to pay the 20% to 35% down payment required by the bank. Doing this will help you to make sure that the people you are getting money from have your best interests at heart and will offer you support toward reaching your financial goal.

You should never get carried away, because using borrowed money can lead to consequences like bankruptcy if things do not go according to plan. If you fail to make a profit from the property you have bought, you might find yourself in financial distress. When you borrow other people's money or get a bank loan, you have a time frame that you are given to pay it back, and if you fail to do so, you might experience an increased interest rate. If you borrowed some of the money from family or friends, you might lose their trust if you fail to pay them back on time.

Now that you have the relevant knowledge about the "plane" method, you can decide if it is well suited for you to reach your financial goal or not. What is most important is to finally reach your destination using a method that will not strain or overly burden you.

Chapter 8:

Get Rich Method 3—The

Rocket

This chapter introduces a method that gives you a faster edge in becoming a millionaire, hence the "rocket" analogy. With the "rocket" method, you can build your wealth by using the power of people and repeatable processes. The "rocket" method is not a get-rich-quick scheme and does present a number of risks, but if done right, you will find yourself on the fast track to becoming a millionaire.

The "rocket" method harnesses elements from the "plane" method, especially the aspects of leveraging. While the "rocket" strategy may also involve leveraging OPM, it goes a step further into using other people's time and skills to accelerate your wealth. You can also take advantage of technology and automation. Basically, the "rocket" method is all about being your own boss. Let's find out more in this chapter.

Leveraging Other People's Time and Skills

Working a regular job means you get paid by the hour, and that limits your earning potential. When you have your own business, you utilize the time and skills of your employees to earn more money. Again, you are still leveraging, just that this time the lever is not the people's money but their time and ability to deliver a service or product.

Let's take the example of a woman named Joana. She works at the local salon as a hairdresser, and her income is calculated on an hourly basis. Joana makes $15 an hour, works eight hours per day, and puts in 40 hours per week. That means in a good week, she earns $600, and in a year, she makes $31,200. If Joana were to open her own salon, she could begin by hiring, say, four hairdressers; so they become five, including herself.

Now, assuming that Joana's employees will earn $15 per hour and work 40 hours a week, each employee earns $600. This means that Joana is giving out wages of $3,000 at the end of every week. Let us say that the customers' hourly cost for the services that Joana's salon provides is $50, and each worker in that salon is occupied with a customer throughout the day. The salon would then have made $10,000 at the end of each week. Let's suppose that Joana pays $1,000 in rent and utilities for the salon weekly. Adding this to the employee's wages ($3,000) means that Joana has to pay a total of $4,000 every week, leaving her with $6,000 in business profits. This amount plus Joana's weekly wages shows that Joana makes $6,600 per week and almost $343,200 per year as her own boss.

The difference between what she would earn as an employee and as the owner of the salon is astounding. Joana's salon business shows that applying the "rocket" method can build your wealth faster than any other plan of action. Salon owners are just one example of how you don't really need to have an extravagant or technological idea to become a millionaire. You can do something as simple as owning a shop or a laundromat and still become successful. You don't really have to develop rockets that fly to Mars like Elon Musk, though there is no harm in doing that if that is what you want to do!

What Are the Risks?

Starting your own business is no easy feat, which could be one of the reasons why many small businesses fail. Creating a business is a gamble, and it can go downhill despite how well you have planned and prepared for it to succeed. Using the "rocket" method means there are high risks coming your way, but if you manage to overcome them, you can reap the high rewards that will follow. Let's explore some of these risks to look out for when starting a business:

- **Financial risk**: Getting your business up and running may require you to funnel in funds from your own savings, family, or investors interested in your project. Cash flow is a big headache in the early stages because you are concerned with how you will pay rent, pay employees, and grow your company. To mitigate this risk, you may have to prepare a well-detailed financial plan outlining your projected income, the figure you will need to break even, and the returns your investors should be expecting once you start turning a profit. When you take time to plan, you help avoid bankruptcy and the failure of your business.

- **Strategic risk**: When your business is still new, you may not have measures in place for decision-making and facing new challenges. The business environment is dynamic and fast-paced. So many changes can occur at any given time that can affect how your business operates. These changes could be due to competition or changes in technology and regulations. The best way to address this risk is through planning and preparing. From your business plan to the staff you hire, work toward mitigating this risk. It also helps to be flexible and keep working toward improvement, because this will maximize your profits and keep you on track to becoming a millionaire.

- **Reputation risk**: Your company's reputation is one of its most valuable assets. Your early stages are where you should make the best impression on your customers. With technological advancements and social media playing a part in the success of your business, you need your consumers to have a lot of good things to say about your product or the service you provide. Managing your reputation has gotten easier and harder at the same time. It's more difficult because every client has a public platform and audience they may use to voice their opinions about your business. Addressing this risk means you should engage with the consumers and respond to feedback. Also, your company should implement a social media policy outlining how staff members should engage with clients and represent the brand on both official and private networks. This will ensure that your staff is aware of the potential consequences that their social media use may have on the business.

- **Liability risk**: When your business is still at a small scale, you might risk being in situations that can lead to unwanted lawsuits and fines. These could be employee or customer injuries, property damages, or failure to meet contractual obligations. You become more vulnerable as a starter business because your liability risk is paired with the reputation risk. The best way to tackle liability risk is to find a good lawyer to handle the legal aspects of your business, as well as an insurance agent to provide your company with the appropriate coverage.

- **Market risk**: The market for a product or service can be impacted by a variety of aspects. Startups are vulnerable to the ups and downs of the economy and emerging market trends, as a particular product can be well-liked one year but not the next. For instance, when the economy is weak, people are less likely to purchase luxury items or non-essentials. If a rival releases a comparable product at a lower cost, the rival might hold a bigger market share. As a new business owner, you should conduct a market analysis that evaluates market variables, consumer demand, and buyer behavior to make sure you are always ahead of the competition.

- **Security risk**: More companies are becoming tech savvy. This puts them at risk of a cyber breach. Cyber security risk can lead to loss of finances, operational disruption, and damage to your reputation. If this threat is not handled well, it can have negative effects on how your company runs and how it is viewed by the public. As a new business owner, one of the best things you can do for your company is to invest in risk management right off the bat.

- **Business interruption risk**: Some events can affect your business flow despite how well you have prepared your strategy and your insurance coverage. Your company may be exposed to natural disasters such as earthquakes, tornadoes, and hurricanes. You may also be vulnerable to wars and recessions. To reduce the effects of such interruptions, you should prepare a business continuity plan to ensure that everything still runs smoothly. This plan will help you keep your customers and reputation intact while also making sure your business does not suffer any losses.

It helps to know these risks, but do not let them prevent you from starting your business. You can manage these risks and keep your company on the right path to success if you stay diligent and proactive. These obstacles do not need to stop you from achieving your goals.

Technology and Automation

It is important that you align your business with advancing technology. Your business will be more flexible and innovative when it moves with the times. Technology in modern-day businesses has played a pivotal role. The internet is the biggest technological tool you can have at your disposal. It will let you sell your product to just about anyone, anywhere in the world. It also gives you an edge when you are hiring employees, as you can save time and vet potential hires based on their digital footprints. Giving your business that technological boost can have a number of benefits:

- **Keeps your business flexible**: Small businesses need to stay in the loop and give rapid responses to customers. This can be achieved using various technological tools. Incorporating technology in your business will keep you ahead of the competition. Your business will grow as a result of faster product launches, better products or services, and improved innovations.

- **Makes collaboration simple**: Coordinating your staff in a new business may not be an easy feat. Communication software has allowed companies to help their employees become more productive. During the COVID-19 pandemic, these software solutions allowed companies to coordinate their employees to work well together in a remote work structure.

- **Improves efficiency**: When you are your own boss, using technology and automated, repeatable processes allows you to be more efficient because the software will do the majority of the work for you and handle the vital tasks better. This will save you time and energy and increase the productivity of your company.

- **Better customer experience**: You want your customers to have a great time so that they will want to come back. Ensure every potential customer has a positive interaction with your business, your products, or the service you provide. Technology can help with this process. You can streamline communication with your customers, collect data to improve the experience, and offer accessibility to your company. Technology can also allow you to better market your company and reach more potential customers. While some rely on newspaper ads, billboards, and signposts, you can take advantage of social media marketing to connect with your target audience. With these tools, you can create a positive relationship with your customers and build your brand image. When compared to more traditional modes of marketing, the digital market provides greater reach at a lower cost.

- **Enhances data security**: Technological tools specific to businesses can help you protect all of your company's sensitive information. Cyber security is a big priority, and tech solutions can help create encryptions and firewalls to protect your business against hackers.

Automating your business will simplify the day-to-day activities in your company. You can use automation to delegate procedures to technology. By leveraging automation for your business, you cut down on labor costs. When you apply technology to your business flow, you reduce the need to hire people. Often, small business owners may hire people for menial tasks that do not benefit the business in the long run but act as an expenditure. Applying technology increases productivity, maximizes your profits, and minimizes the occurrence of human error.

Make a Business out of Your Passion

When you take the time to build your company around what you already love, you will have the enthusiasm and resilience your business needs to succeed. You create something you are happy with and will be proud to leave as a legacy for your children and their children. Being your own boss allows you to create fulfillment instead of chasing it. You get to do what you want and like, for the rest of your life. You have complete control over every facet of your business, the goods or services you offer, marketing, and sales tactics.

If you have a passion for art, why not create a business along those lines? Are you a passionate cook, baker, hairdresser, fashion designer, or makeup artist? If yes, then it's time to break the limits and earn more from what you truly love doing. Let's dive into the steps that you need to follow to build your business around your passion:

- **Define your vision**: Knowing where you want to be is the center of starting a business. Make a well-defined vision statement that will keep you on the path to achieving your goals. As your company grows and you add team members and structure to your organization, this vision statement will serve as a regular reminder of your company's objectives.

- **Do your research**: Learn everything you can about starting your business. Understand your market, the clientele you want to attract, and the competition you will face once you start. Thorough research will identify the risks your business will face and allow you to plan for how you will manage them. You can also use this step to find the market gap, and how following your passion will fill it. Reach out to others who have found success in your field and gain knowledge from how they did it.

- **Make a plan**: Without a well-organized and concise strategic plan for how you're going to get your business up and running, your vision cannot become a reality. A business plan needs to be adaptive, digestible, and measurable in order to start things moving. It must be adaptive since conditions change constantly and you will need to go with the flow. As a boss, you need to educate your employees on the plan. Be sure to make your plan measurable so that you can track progress.

- **Be aware of your finances**: How will you fund your startup? You have a variety of options, including raising money, obtaining a loan, obtaining a credit card, creating an account, and using your own savings. Plan and be sure of the income sources that will keep your business going, especially during its infant stages.

- **Test drive your passion**: It is best to start your business small. This will assist you in assessing the viability of the business before you scale up too big. When you start small, you minimize your mistakes, and if there are any, they are easier to correct.

- **Keep your nine-to-five**: Starting your business while enjoying the stability and safety of your day job is the ideal method to eventually convert passion into profit. You should hold onto your full-time job until your passion project is bringing in a steady stream of income that is close to your current salary or even more.

- **Build an online presence**: Your business needs a website. Creating one allows you to communicate your passion to the rest of the world. This may also foster brand loyalty. Additionally, a website can make running your business so much easier.

- **Think long-term**: Once your startup is up and running, you should give yourself time to look into the big picture. Is your business going in a way that allows you to expand? I am renting now, but will I be able to acquire a permanent residence for my company? These are the kinds of questions you should ask yourself if you are thinking about your business succeeding well into the future.

Once you have found your passion and followed all these steps, the next thing for you would be to turn your business into a thriving enterprise. Don't go at it alone; look for help from mentors, systems, freelancers, and even just family and friends. Create a team to help your business have every relevant skill set at its disposal. Owning a small business is hard work, but, as the saying goes, "If you do what you love, you never work a day in your life."

Advantages and Disadvantages of the "Rocket" Method

The "rocket" method does come with a few disadvantages, which include the following:

- It can be risky, as many new businesses fail.

- It can (and often will) take a lot of your time.

- Depending on the industry you want to dive into, it may need significant capital to start.

However, this strategy also has the following benefits that might make you change your mind:

- You get to be your own boss.

- You set your own hours.

- You get to be as creative as you want with your business.

- You have the potential for explosive growth once your business takes off.

Ultimately, using the "rocket" method will still require you to be hands-on with your finances, even if you have a network of professionals helping you at each step. The most important thing is to not give up on your goals when it starts getting hard. With patience and resilience, you have the potential to reap significant rewards from your hard work.

Chapter 9:

Which "Get Rich" Method Is Best for You? Your "Get Rich" Personal Assessment

Now that you know the three vehicles to your million-dollar financial destination, which "get rich" method are you going to start with? To spare you the confusion, this chapter will help you to determine whether you should use a train, plane, or rocket to get started on your journey to accumulating wealth. While plenty of millionaires get rich by using various combinations of the three strategies, they all started with a first step. You also need to find your starting point. Therefore, the purpose of this chapter is to help you to decide which "get rich" method aligns with your personality, style, and goals.

The Assessment

The procedure for determining your best possible "get rich" method involves providing you with a series of questions that you should honestly answer by circling either the 0 or 1. Alongside each question, there will be hints that guide you on how you might allocate your marks. The method that does not apply to you at any given time will get zero marks, while those that are potentially suitable get a mark each. Please note that mark allocation is done on the small table that is below each question. You will then have to add the marks for each method at the end of the assessment. The "get rich" method with the highest marks is the one you may want to consider as your first step for now. Let's get started!

1. Do you have poor credit that would prevent you from getting a mortgage in the event that you want to buy real estate? **Hint:** If yes, then the "plane" method isn't the best option for now. The "train" and "rocket" strategies might work better.

Train		Plane		Rocket	
0	1	0	1	0	1

2. Do you have enough money to use as a downpayment on a real estate property? **Hint:** If not, the "plane" method won't work at the moment. The "train" and "rocket" methods might work with what you have at your disposal.

Train		Plane		Rocket	
0	1	0	1	0	1

3. Is your schedule so busy that you have *zero* time available for managing real estate or another business? **Hint:** If yes, then the "plane" and "rocket" are not the best options because they are usually more time-consuming. You don't need to set aside much time for the "train" method, which is more of a hands-off strategy of getting rich.

Train		Plane		Rocket	
0	1	0	1	0	1

4. Do you have some time, money for a downpayment, and decent credit? **Hint:** If yes, the "plane" might be the way to go. The other methods also work for you because you have some money to start with.

Train		Plane		Rocket	
0	1	0	1	0	1

5. Are you young and working? **Hint:** If yes, then you have more time ahead so all methods are applicable, even the "train" method.

Train		Plane		Rocket	
0	1	0	1	0	1

6. Are you older, with the desire to get rich at a faster pace, yet you have little money? **Hint:** If yes, starting a business, that is, the "rocket" method, could be the best possible option.

Train		Plane		Rocket	
0	1	0	1	0	1

7. Do you have a brilliant idea that could solve certain problems in communities and have some savings to fund your business idea? **Hint:** If yes, you could consider starting a business and hop on the "rocket." If there is a business gap that can be covered by real estate investing in your target area, then the "plane" might also work, as long as you have all the necessary requirements.

Train		Plane		Rocket	
0	1	0	1	0	1

8. Do you have a passion that you can turn into a business, and though you don't have much money, you have other options for funding the idea? **Hint:** If yes, you could go for the "rocket" strategy of getting rich.

Train		Plane		Rocket	
0	1	0	1	0	1

9. Do you prefer a method of accumulating wealth that requires fewer skills? **Hint:** If yes, then that cannot be a "plane" or a "rocket." You will have to go for the "train" because this strategy can be used by anyone, regardless of the type or level of education that they possess.

Train		Plane		Rocket	
0	1	0	1	0	1

10. Do you feel excited at the thought of becoming your own boss and that of others? **Hint:** If yes, things could work well for you if you use the "rocket" method. Real estate investing can also bring about similar feelings, so you might also want to try the "plane" method.

Train		Plane		Rocket	
0	1	0	1	0	1

11. Do you want a "get rich" method that requires the lowest amount of money to start, even without credit? **Hint:** If yes, then that might be the "train" strategy.

Train		Plane		Rocket	
0	1	0	1	0	1

12. Are you not in so much of a hurry to make your money? **Hint:** If yes, the "train" method works, though you also have the leverage to use the other strategies as long as you qualify.

Train		Plane		Rocket	
0	1	0	1	0	1

13. Do you feel that you are an entrepreneur and have the ability to chart your own course? **Hint:** If yes, you can make money using the "rocket" method.

Train		Plane		Rocket	
0	1	0	1	0	1

14. Are you in a scenario where you don't have money at the moment, yet you want to get started immediately? **Hint:** If yes, you can go with the "rocket" if you find a business idea that can be started with no money. The other methods will certainly require some monetary input on your side.

Train		Plane		Rocket	
0	1	0	1	0	1

15. Do you have some prior knowledge of or some education in subjects that are related to the real estate industry? **Hint:** If yes, then why not go for the "plane" strategy?

Train		Plane		Rocket	
0	1	0	1	0	1

16. Are you emotionally stable enough to face the risks that are involved in investing? **Hint:** If not, going for "train"

is not so much of a good idea because you could lose all or part of your money. Starting a business is also associated with risk because there are some ideas that flop. You can only bear that if you can better manage your emotions.

Train		Plane		Rocket	
0	1	0	1	0	1

17. Have you laid a strong financial foundation by mastering the basics of personal finance, such as budgeting and living within your means? **Hint:** If not, then none of the three "get rich" methods will likely work for you in the long run. You should be able to manage your personal finances properly before you can handle more complicated math that is associated with bigger amounts of money.

Train		Plane		Rocket	
0	1	0	1	0	1

18. Do you feel comfortable working with a bank or other lending institution for you to start making or growing your money? **Hint:** If yes, then the "plane" might be the way to go, considering that they quite often are willing to make loans for real estate properties. This is because the

banks are more likely to get a loan repaid when it is based on historically more stable long-term investments such as real estate.

Train		Plane		Rocket	
0	1	0	1	0	1

19. Do you think you can take advantage of technology, automation, and the internet to make more money? **Hint:** If yes, you can consider the "rocket" method. This strategy leverages technology and automation to increase productivity, hence giving the potential to make more profit.

Train		Plane		Rocket	
0	1	0	1	0	1

20. Do you prefer a scenario where you grow your money by compound interest, without much of your input? **Hint:** If yes, the "train" method is a good way to achieve that. The "plane" strategy partly offers this benefit if you

Train		Plane		Rocket	
0	1	0	1	0	1

are using real estate investment groups.

21. Are you looking for a venture through which you can grow your money without having to go out of your way to fund it? **Hint:** The "train" method provides you with that advantage. You regularly save a preset amount that you can afford every month. If you can start a business that requires little to no money to begin with, you can also go for the "rocket" method.

Train		Plane		Rocket	
0	1	0	1	0	1

22. What are the time frames during which you want to raise your first $1 million? **Hint:** The shorter the period, the more you need faster methods such as the "plane" or even the "rocket." If you set a longer time frame, the "train" will also work.

Train		Plane		Rocket	
0	1	0	1	0	1

23. Have you determined your risk tolerance levels yet? **Hint:** If not, then you can't venture into any of the methods, considering that all of them are associated with a certain level of risk. However, if you did, you can go for the "rocket," "plane," or bigger investments in the "train" if you trust your emotional stability. If not,

investing small amounts using the "train" method could be the way to go.

Train		Plane		Rocket	
0	1	0	1	0	1

24. Do you want to use other people's money as a way to accelerate the growth of your wealth? **Hint:** If yes, you can go for the "plane."

Train		Plane		Rocket	
0	1	0	1	0	1

25. Do you prefer a money-making venture that has increased variety in terms of what can be done? **Hints:** You can never go wrong with the "plane" in this case. Remember you can deal in property rentals, house flipping, or real estate investment groups, depending on your preferences.

Train		Plane		Rocket	
0	1	0	1	0	1

26. Do you feel that you want to use your skills in making money toward your goal of becoming a millionaire? **Hint:** If yes, the "rocket" method will give you ample opportunity to exercise your skills and make money from them. If your skills are oriented toward real estate investing and you have what it takes to start the venture, the "plane" will also work for you.

Train		Plane		Rocket	
0	1	0	1	0	1

27. Do you need a money-making method where not everything solely depends on you? **Hint:** The "plane" and "rocket" methods can offer this advantage. With these methods, you can hire people who can take up some responsibilities so some tasks can be performed even in your absence. For example, in real estate investments, you can hire a manager to oversee your rental properties. In the "rocket" strategy, collaborating with others and bringing in other people who have skills such as accounting will take your money-making venture to another level.

Train		Plane		Rocket	
0	1	0	1	0	1

28. Is enjoying the process of making or growing your money one of your main priorities? **Hint:** If yes, then you have to go with something that aligns with your passion. This is possible with the "rocket" method. If you have a passion for real estate investing, then the "plane" method might be your best pick.

Train		Plane		Rocket	
0	1	0	1	0	1

29. Do you enjoy working with people? **Hint:** The "plane" and "rocket" methods involve working with people. Therefore, you will want to have good people and communication skills. This is less of an issue when you are using the "train" method of getting rich.

Train		Plane		Rocket	
0	1	0	1	0	1

The questions that you have just gone through are only there to guide your decision with regard to the "get rich" method that you will start with. Based on the answers that you gave, find the sum of the marks that you got for each strategy. The one that has the highest number of marks is the one you may want to consider as your starting point. You may also want to see if there is much of a difference between the methods that would have taken the first and second positions. If there isn't much of a difference, the "number two" could be the next possible option when you decide to expand your horizons after establishing the "number one" choice.

So, at this point, you now have your "why," your "belief" in yourself, and the method to start with, along with an understanding of what those methods are. This presents us with a good transition to the last chapter of this book, which will guide you on the next steps to get started.

Chapter 10:

Practical Next Steps to Get

Started

According to Wayne Gretzky, "You miss 100% of the shots that you don't take" (Gretzky, n.d.). This quote explains the fact that winning can only happen when you play the game. So, no matter how much knowledge you accumulate, not taking action is more or less the same as "not taking the shots that you should have." This is why we compiled this action-oriented chapter for you to review immediately after learning about the three "get rich" strategies. In this chapter, we will present to you some steps you should consider taking once you have selected the method that you will start with. This means that by the time you reach the end of this chapter, you will be in a better position to get started. We, therefore, give you the mandate to take that first step within the next 24 hours. Take your shot!

Next Steps for the "Train" Method

Let's look at the next steps that you can take if the vehicle to your first $1 million is the "train."

Self-Directed Investing Account Versus Working With a Professional Advisor

When you are investing, you can either use a self-directed brokerage account or employ the services of a professional advisor. With a self-directed method, you are responsible for managing your money by yourself. On the contrary, when your account is "managed," your investment advisor has input into the investment of your money. As you start out with the "train" method, it can be difficult to determine whether to self-manage your account or to work with a professional advisor. The information that we will discuss here will make it easier for you to make your choice.

Advantages and Disadvantages of a Self-Directed Account

The advantages of a self-directed account include the following:

- The involved costs are typically lower, considering that you won't need to pay the professional advisor.

- How your funds are allocated is solely your decision to make. You, therefore, take full responsibility for what happens in your account.

- You may have increased flexibility through a wider range of investment options.

The disadvantages of managing your brokerage account on your own are as follows:

- Personally managing your account can sometimes result in less diversification. Such a scenario causes you to suffer great losses in the event that you make a bad decision. In contrast, the greater diversification that often comes with managed accounts spreads the risk across many investments.

- When you manage your account by yourself, emotions can easily control your decision-making ability. So, you are more likely to act in response to what you feel, and this can lead to wrong moves being made.

- By managing your account on your own, you forgo the golden opportunity to get professional advice that enhances your ability to come up with a viable and effective investment strategy.

- Managing your own account is a time-consuming endeavor because you have to be logging in every now and then to check on how things are going.

Advantages and Disadvantages of a Managed Account

Here are some of the advantages that are associated with a managed account:

- You get access to expert management for your account, thereby increasing the chances for success.

- Having someone else manage your investments reduces emotional decision-making.

- You are saved from the responsibility of making hard and tricky decisions pertaining to your investments.

Here are some disadvantages:

- The services of a professional advisor typically come at an extra cost.

- You may give up some control over your investments, as your advisor will be providing guidance and recommendations.

How Much and When to Start Saving

Another important aspect is knowing when to start saving and how much you should put aside. This has to be predetermined before you start the saving procedure. Saving based on a stipulated and logical calculation gives you more discipline toward the endeavor, as compared to just saving randomly. In this section, we will explain one method that can provide some guidance on the amount that you may want to save.

The 50-30-20 Rule

Talking about actual values can be difficult since we all have different amounts of income, spending patterns, and responsibilities. However, the 50-30-20 rule can be used by everyone in a relatively fair manner because it uses percentages, not actual monetary values. The 50-30-20 rule helps you to calculate how much of your income you may want to spend, and the amount that you may want to channel toward saving. Let's see how this rule works.

Half, which is 50% of your income, is a reasonable amount to be allocated to catering to your needs. Such needs include your rent, food, work wardrobe, and gas for your car, among other things. Then, 30% of the total income is what you might use for any form of fun. This could be eating out, traveling, and family outings. The final 20% is what you could then channel toward savings for future use. Some experts suggest that if you are a beginner in the world of saving, 20% could be difficult, so they suggest that if that's the case, starting with 1% could be a better idea. You can then gradually increase until you hit the 20% mark.

You can start saving any time. In this case, we recommend that you start now to avoid procrastination. Remember that "procrastination is the thief of time."

Open a Savings or Investment Account

There are different types of savings accounts, and your choice of which one to open mainly depends on your end goal. You might also need to consider whether you want a savings account from which you can withdraw funds or one where you just continue to make deposits for long periods of time. Here are some of the types of savings accounts that you can choose from:

- **Standard savings accounts**: You will find this type at many credit unions and banks.

- **High-yield savings accounts**: Although you may find this type of savings account in brick-and-mortar banks, they are mainly available in online credit unions and banks. Here, the annual percentage yields (APY) are higher.

- **Money market funds**: These accounts allow you to deposit money into your account and then withdraw it whenever you need it.

- **Certificates of deposit (CD)**: In this case, you deposit your money and leave it there for a predetermined amount of time. During that time, your money earns a fixed interest.

- **Specialty savings accounts**: The money that you deposit in these accounts is saved toward specific goals or people. For example, you could save for children's school fees.

How to Open a Savings Account

You can open a savings account in four simple steps as follows:

1. **Have your details and documentation handy**: Irrespective of whether you open your account in person or online, you should have the following documents available: date of birth, government issued ID, Social Security Number, email address, and mailing address.

2. **Select the account category**: You have the option to open a single or joint account. If you want a joint account, the co-signer will have to be there, along with their own documentation.

3. **Pay the initial deposit**: You might be asked to pay a minimum deposit in some cases, so be prepared. You can pay cash deposits in brick-and-mortar banks, but online ones may give you some other deposit options. It is also possible to transfer funds from a bank account that is linked to the savings account.

4. **Submit**: Before you make your submission, don't forget to accept the terms and conditions of the bank. After the bank has accepted your application, you can start making deposits to your savings account.

Set Up an Automatic Monthly Contribution

Setting an automatic transfer to the savings account takes away the burden of having to think about when and how much to transfer to your savings account. You also eliminate the chances of forgetting to make the transfer.

This task is relatively simple. All you have to do is to determine the amount of money that you want to transfer from the linked bank account to your savings account after a predetermined period, which is a month in this case. Now, schedule an automatic deposit of that amount to your savings account. Remember to make it recurring so that the deposit is automatically made every month. Ideally, you can schedule your deposit to be done a week after you get your paycheck so that you give it ample time to clear. However, it's not really the time of deposit that matters most when it comes to automatic monthly contributions; it's the consistency that is more important.

Please note that it is also possible to make automatic deposits from a CD account to an individual retirement account.

Next Steps for the "Plane" Method

In this section, we will highlight the next steps that you should take if the "plane" method is the one that you will start with.

Build Your Team

You will need a formidable team to work with in real estate investing. To put together such a great team, be sure to conduct thorough interviews. Also, do background checks on potential candidates. It is also important for you to get relevant references and seek more information from the employers and clients who previously worked with the candidates. All this is necessary so that you avoid working with the wrong people, a scenario that might be costly to you in terms of money and time.

What kind of people do you need on your team to begin with? Here is a list that can help:

- lawyer
- banker
- realtor
- accountant
- cleaning company
- electrician
- handyman
- bookkeeper
- administrative assistant

Identify Source of Funds for Down Payment

Since the bank will not give you all the money that you need to purchase property, you must have money that is set aside for a down payment. You have to be clear on how you intend to raise that money. Here are some ideas:

- **Savings**: If you have enough money in your savings account, you can use that to make your down payment.

- **Angel inventors**: Angel investors are people who fund small businesses or businesses that are just starting.

- **Family and friends**: Getting money from your friends and family is another form of OPM. This option is especially good for small businesses that will need financing for a long period of time. One of the advantages of this type of OPM is that it often does not require you to give up a percentage of your ownership stake.

- **Loan**: You can apply for loans from banks, microfinance institutions, and credit and savings societies. Keep in mind, however, that loans come with interest rates.

- **Silent partners**: A "silent partner" is a person that you involve in your property ownership, and your partnership is based on that individual's ability to provide capital. A silent partner rarely gets involved in the property's day-to-day operations. In some instances, the silent partner does not even attend management meetings.

- **Crowdfunding**: Crowdfunding occurs when a group of people come together and all contribute money that will be pooled and used to fund a project. This is basically a network of investors and entrepreneurs who are connected through social media. Crowdfunding has restrictions when it comes to who is allowed to contribute. Crowdfunding gives investors the choice of choosing the type of project to fund, and they can contribute as little as 10 dollars. There are a number of crowdfunding sites that you can use to get access to funds; these include GoFundMe, Kickstarter, and Indiegogo.

Familiarize Yourself With Optimal Locations

Have you already identified the area where you are going to purchase your first property? If yes, you need to know more about that location. You need to know where the closest schools, hospitals, and universities are located. You can also do research on the safety and crime levels in that location. What is the general cost of the houses that are found in that area? These are just ideas, but there is a lot that you can find out in a bid to know more about the location.

Find Out the Rental Vacancy Rates of Relevant Locations

The vacancy rates describe the number of unoccupied units in a property that is available for renting, presented as a percentage. Therefore, to calculate the vacancy rate, use this formula:

[(Number of vacant units)/(Total number of available units)] x 100

Generally, when the vacancy rates in your target location are higher, this is an indication that the properties there are not renting out so well, which is a disadvantage to you as an investor.

Contrastingly, lower vacancy rates are associated with a potentially better business for you as an investor.

Next Steps for the "Rocket" Method

In this section, we will look at the next steps that you should take if the "rocket" method is your first choice for starting your journey to your first million.

Identify Your Business Idea

As we highlighted earlier, you should identify a business gap that you can fill with your idea. For example, if you realize that there is no tailor around a certain location, you might decide to fill in that gap by starting a tailoring business. Your business idea may be fueled by the interest, knowledge, skills, or passion that you have, so be ready to think outside the box.

Do Some Research

Once you have established an idea, the next thing is to do quality research to see if you can earn profits from it. Mind you, there is no point in setting up a business that offers services or products that no one is willing to pay for. This is why market research is very important. You also want to find out what your competitors who are already in the market are offering. You will need to do the SWOT analysis to get this done effectively. SWOT is an acronym for strengths, weaknesses, opportunities, and threats. It analyzes these factors in relation to your competitors so that you can identify opportunities for excelling in the market.

Develop a Business Plan

You will want to have a business plan for your venture. A business plan is both an outline and forecast that presents how your business will be run. It is an overview of what your business is all about. The business plan covers the administration, operational, and financial aspects of your business. With a well-drafted business plan in place, you have the roadmap for the next one or so years of your business. Please note that your business plan should highlight how you intend to fund your business before it reaches the break-even point.

Register Your Business

Depending on your location and type of business, you may be required to register your business and potentially obtain permits. Check with your local authorities as to what is required in your area.

Think of Protecting Your Business

After all the hard work and input that you invest in your business, protecting it is justified. Therefore, you will want to strongly consider getting the appropriate business insurance coverage. Some of the coverages that you may consider are

- General liability insurance: This shields your company from liability claims that involve property damage and bodily injury.

- Professional liability coverage: This insurance covers you in case you are sued for negligence that is associated with your service provision.

- Business income insurance: This assists you to replace your income in the event of mishaps such as fires and natural disasters.

Promote Your Business

It's time to make your business known to people who need its products and/or services. You will need to come up with a strategic market plan for this to work. You might also need to create a website, in addition to establishing an online presence through social media. Take advantage of platforms such as Facebook and Twitter for advertising. Creating blogs and YouTube videos are other options that you may want to explore as well. When you create YouTube videos and blogs, we recommend that you use search engine optimization (SEO) to increase the chances of attracting the right audience.

Activity

One thing that you should do within the next 24 hours is decide on which of the three methods you will use. For help with getting started, you can go to https://dsp.pub/getrichresources for a free resources page we have provided.

This resources page will provide you with additional helpful information and practical step-by-step guides you can follow to help turn your "get rich" dream into a reality. Taking the next step (soon), even if it is a small step, is critically important. By doing this, you become more committed to moving forward.

Conclusion: Today Is the First Day of the Rest of Your Life

Let me ask you a direct question: If you don't take the steps necessary to improve your situation, who will? The truth is that nobody else will. If you are hesitating, then you need to ask yourself: Are your "whys" for taking action not more important than your "why nots"?

This book took you through the process of identifying your "why" so that you can find the motivation to tackle any obstacles that you come across along your way to making your first $1 million. Your "whys" will keep you focused on your financial goal. We then went on to identify your "why nots," which are the obstacles that you are more likely to see the moment you take your eyes off your goals. After becoming acquainted with your "whys" and "why nots," the next step is to work on building your self-esteem. In the same way that high self-confidence contributes to achieving other goals, so it is with making money.

We then moved from the more person-oriented chapters of the book and began the transition to more technical aspects. To get this done, we used the chapter on laying a good foundation of personal finance basics as the transitional message. We then delved into the three "get rich" methods that you can use as vehicles for your first $1 million. These are saving and investing, described as the "train"; using OPM, described as the "plane"; and using the incredible power of people and repeatable processes, also known as the "rocket." Having dished out the three vehicles to becoming a millionaire, we then provided you with an assessment that helped you to identify the "get rich" method that you will start with before you begin thinking of employing multiple methods for faster results.

Now that you have a basic framework that you can use to accumulate wealth, all that is missing is the most important ingredient: *you*! You simply need to motivate yourself so that you can start taking the necessary action as presented in Chapter 10 of this book.

Take a moment of silence and get into a moment of imagination. Make sure there are little to no distractions around to derail your focus. Now, imagine what your life would look like if you were to take action and, like so many others, achieve this level of financial freedom. What would your days look like? Are they going to be more peaceful and less stressful? Will you be in a position where you can afford most of the things that you desire? Maybe you will also be in a better position to assist your loved ones the way you couldn't before. Now, come back to your current self and remember that so many people just like you have been able to achieve their financial freedom using the same methods that are described in this book. It isn't necessary to have expert knowledge or to be the best, brightest, strongest, most beautiful, and so on. What it's really about is just you making a decision to do something and then taking the needed steps, one at a time, to make it happen.

The most important step in your journey is the "next one." We encourage you to take that step, knowing that as you do so, you will be approaching your desired financial destination. And please let us know about your success stories and how you are doing. We'd love to hear from you!

And if you've found the book helpful and encouraging, we'd love it if you would visit https://dsp.pub/getrichreview to leave us a review.

Good luck!

Thank You!

Thank you for reading my book! I've worked really hard on my book and would love your feedback. Please visit https://dsp.pub/getrichreview to leave a review.

As an independent author, your kind reviews help so much. I read every review and sincerely appreciate your feedback!

References

Admin. (2020, February 13). *Managed account or self-directed brokerage account – which is for you?* Sarwa. https://www.sarwa.co/blog/managed-account-or-self-directed-brokerage-account-which-is-for-you-2

AFG. (n.d.). *This guide has received the label in medium-and long-term investment solutions 12 principles for saving and investing.* https://www.afg.asso.fr/wp-content/uploads/2021/02/afg-financial-education-12-principles.pdf

AICPA. (n.d.). *6 tips for living without credit cards.* 360 Degrees of Financial Literacy. https://www.360financialliteracy.org/Topics/Credit-and-Debt/Credit-Cards-and-Reports/6-Tips-for-Living-without-Credit-Cards

Balfour, B., & Matthews, K. L. (2022, July 29). *How bad credit affects you.* LendingTree. https://www.lendingtree.com/credit-repair/how-bad-credit-affects-you/

Bennett, K. (2022, December 13). *Emergency fund: What it is and how to start one.* Bankrate. https://www.bankrate.com/banking/savings/starting-an-emergency-fund/

Bigger Pockets. (2019, December 8). *The 7 indispensable team members of a property management company.* Biggerpockets.com.

https://www.biggerpockets.com/blog/team-members-property-management

Boogaard, K. (2021, December 26). *Write achievable goals with the SMART goals framework*. Work Life by Atlassian; Atlassian. https://www.atlassian.com/blog/productivity/how-to-write-smart-goals

Brown, M. (2022, July 15). *Get enough sleep*. Health.gov. https://health.gov/myhealthfinder/healthy-living/mental-health-and-relationships/get-enough-sleep

Burnette, M. (2022, August 17). *How to open a savings account: Step by step*. NerdWallet. https://www.nerdwallet.com/article/banking/how-to-open-a-savings-account-step-by-step

Cabral, C. (2020, July 23). *7 mental obstacles to getting rich and how to beat them*. Shortform Books. https://www.shortform.com/blog/mental-obstacles-rich-dad-poor-dad/

Caldwell, M. (2021, November 28). *Understanding budgeting and personal finance*. The Balance. https://www.thebalancemoney.com/personal-finance-budget-4802696

Çam, D. (2017, October 18). *Doctorate, degree or dropout: How much education it takes to become a billionaire*. Forbes. https://www.forbes.com/sites/denizcam/2017/10/18/doctorate-degree-or-dropout-how-much-education-it-takes-to-become-a-billionaire/?sh=2b2284a0b044

CDC. (2022, April 27). *Benefits of physical activity*. Centers for Disease Control and Prevention; CDC. https://www.cdc.gov/physicalactivity/basics/pa-health/index.htm

Chang, D. (2022, June 7). *3 in 4 millionaires say this is key to financial success*. The Motley Fool. https://www.fool.com/the-ascent/buying-stocks/articles/3-in-4-millionaires-say-this-is-key-to-financial-success/

Chi, C. (2022, April 8). *5 dos and don'ts when making a SMART goal*. Blog.hubspot.com. https://blog.hubspot.com/marketing/smart-goal-examples

Collier, G. (2019, July 17). *Destroy your debt in 10 (not-so-easy) steps*. Moneyweb. https://www.moneyweb.co.za/financial-advisor-views/destroy-your-debt-in-10-not-so-easy-steps/

Community Health Network. (2022, March 17). *4 reasons why sleep is good for your health*. Access Community Health Network. https://www.achn.net/about-access/whats-new/health-resources/4-reason-why-sleep-is-good-for-your-health/

Corley, T. (2022, July 31). *I spent 5 years interviewing 225 millionaires. Here are the 4 types of rich people and their top habits*. CNBC. https://www.cnbc.com/2022/07/31/i-spent-5-years-interviewing-225-millionaires-3-money-habits-that-helped-them-get-rich.html

Edison, T. (n.d.). *I have gotten a lot of results! I know several thousand things that won't work*. Quote Investigator.

https://quoteinvestigator.com/2012/07/31/edison-lot-results/

Elkins, K. (2017). Rich people use these 6 mental tricks to make more money. *CNBC.* https://www.cnbc.com/2017/03/29/11-thoughts-that-could-be-holding-you-back-from-financial-success.html

Elkins, K. (2019, July 22). *Sallie Krawcheck: Use this simple formula to figure out how much money you should save and spend.* CNBC. https://www.cnbc.com/2019/07/22/use-the-50-30-20-formula-to-figure-out-how-much-you-should-save.html

Fearless Motivation. (2017, September 11). *15 of the best motivational quotes by great athletes on struggle and success.* Fearless Motivation - Motivational Videos and Music. https://www.fearlessmotivation.com/2017/09/13/motivational-quotes-by-athletes/

Foundation Repair. (2020, April 10). *Extreme example of foundation failure.* Structured Foundation Repairs. https://www.structuredfoundation.com/blog/extreme-example-of-foundation-failure/

Garcia, M. C. (2022, September 28). *How to open a savings account.* Forbes Advisor. www.forbes.com. https://www.forbes.com/advisor/banking/savings/how-to-open-savings-account/

Gretzky, W. (n.d.). *Wayne Gretzky quotes.* BrainyQuote. https://www.brainyquote.com/quotes/wayne_gretzky_378694

Grossman, A. L. (2010, January 28). *Why I want to be rich (also, why do people want to be rich)?* Frugal Confessions - How

to Save Money.
https://www.frugalconfessions.com/save-me-
money/why-do-i-want-to-be-rich/

Hall, J. (2021, January 19). *Average stock market return*. The
Motley Fool. https://www.fool.com/investing/how-to-
invest/stocks/average-stock-market-return/

Harrison, C. (2018, July 13). *Top 10 richest dropouts in the world.*
Salary.com. https://www.salary.com/articles/top-10-
richest-dropouts-in-the-world/

Kahneman, D., & Deaton, A. (2010). High Income Improves
Evaluation of Life but Not Emotional Well-Being.
Proceedings of the National Academy of Sciences, 107(38),
16489–16493.
https://doi.org/10.1073/pnas.1011492107

Kiyosaki, R. (2012, September 16). *Rich dad, poor dad - Chapter 8.*
Network Tambayan.
https://networktambayan.weebly.com/robert-
kiyosakis-rich-dad-poor-dad/rich-dad-poor-dad-
chapter-8

Kumok, Z. (2022, September 16). *5 ways to get out of debt.*
Bankrate. https://www.bankrate.com/personal-
finance/debt/ways-to-get-out-of-debt/

Lake, R. (2022, October 19). *Budgets: Everything you need to know.*
The Balance.
https://www.thebalancemoney.com/how-to-make-a-
budget-1289587

Lisa, A. (2022, July 20). *10 habits of self-made millionaires that could
make you rich*. Yahoo Finance.
https://finance.yahoo.com/news/10-habits-self-made-

millionaires-
150001505.html?guccounter=1&guce_referrer=aHR0c
HM6Ly93d3cuZ29vZ2xlLmNvbS88&guce_referrer_sig
=AQAAAFlJoiXLVe4nPO9f6lc6aaaitty_8ituqEqL9W
HeoIjQuLw9Wpu9yg8R_2fhzOlDIxdPdtMaO1k-
wjpB5V-
mS7EXOWXIwI9olTuX1aOHx9ioQeyy0TJj5MiJw-
2ckth6eUif7kAGw_Bi9aEXbI-
_taIKvnhwb4jFfdUgoD-_WEDc

Luthar, S. S. (2003). The culture of affluence: psychological costs of material wealth. *Child Development*, *74*(6), 1581–1593. https://doi.org/10.1046/j.1467-8624.2003.00625.x

Martin, A. (2019, June 11). *How to survive and thrive without a credit card*. Forbes Advisor. https://www.forbes.com/advisor/credit-cards/how-to-survive-and-thrive-without-a-credit-card/

McCain, A. (2022a, October 10). *33 Millionaire statistics: 8.8% Of US adults are millionaires*. Zippia. https://www.zippia.com/advice/millionaire-statistics/

McGurran, B. (2019, July 29). *How to "fix" a bad credit score*. Experian. https://www.experian.com/blogs/ask-experian/credit-education/improving-credit/how-to-fix-a-bad-credit-score/

Merle, A. (2017, October 5). *The sleep routines of successful people*. Medium. https://andrewmerle.medium.com/the-sleep-routines-of-successful-people-35d847249ce1

NHS. (2022, February 23). *Facts about fat*. Nhs.uk. https://www.nhs.uk/live-well/eat-well/food-types/different-fats-nutrition/

Olson, E. J. (2021, May 15). *How many hours of sleep do you need?* Mayo Clinic. https://www.mayoclinic.org/healthy-lifestyle/adult-health/expert-answers/how-many-hours-of-sleep-are-enough/faq-20057898

Personal Finance. (n.d.). *5 steps to build an emergency fund.* Securian Financial. https://www.securian.com/insights-tools/articles/5-steps-to-building-an-emergency-fund.html

Rampton, J. (2017, November 21). *9 obstacles you must overcome to make your first million.* Entrepreneur. https://www.entrepreneur.com/leadership/9-obstacles-you-must-overcome-to-make-your-first-million/305011

Resource Pages https://dsp.pub/getrichresources

Rohde, J. (n.d.). *What is the vacancy rate and how should you calculate it?* Stessa. https://www.stessa.com/blog/vacancy-rate/

Roland, J. (2022, January 25). *Sleep calculator: How many hours and sleep cycles do you need?* Healthline. https://www.healthline.com/health/sleep/sleep-calculator

Royal, J. (2023, January 25). *Saving versus investing: Key differences and when to choose.* Bankrate. https://www.bankrate.com/investing/saving-vs-investing/

Sara. (2018, February 7). *Why do you want to be rich? 10 things people work for.* JewelPie. https://jewelpie.com/why-do-you-want-to-be-rich-10-things-people-work-for/

Seeker, F. (2019, August 2). *9 reasons you should want to be rich*. Striving for Felicity. https://strivingforfelicity.com/9-reasons-you-should-want-to-be-rich/

Sethi, R. (2021, May 24). *Why do you want to be rich?* I Will Teach You to Be Rich. https://www.iwillteachyoutoberich.com/blog/why-do-you-want-to-be-rich/

Sheroes. (2019, June 28). *Women who proved that failure is the path to success*. Sheroes.com. https://sheroes.com/articles/women-who-proved-that-failure-is-the-path-to-success/MTQyODY=

Sightings, T. (2018). *7 myths about millionaires*. US News & World Report; U.S. News & World Report. https://money.usnews.com/money/blogs/on-retirement/articles/7-myths-about-millionaires

Study.com. (2022). *Occupancy and vacancy analysis: Definition and process*. Study.com. https://study.com/academy/lesson/occupancy-vacancy-analysis-definition-process.html

Taleb, H. (2018, May 5). *Proven steps to set goals like Napoleon Hill*. Medium. https://medium.com/@husseintaleb/proven-steps-to-set-goals-like-napoleon-hill-f6d7162c40f6

Tessler, B. (2016, September 30). *4 grounded ways to marry money and spirituality*. Bari Tessler. https://baritessler.com/2016/09/4-grounded-ways-marry-money-spirituality/

Watkins, B. (2019, March 13). *Thomas Edison's Theorem for success*. CRY Magazine. https://medium.com/cry-

mag/thomas-edisons-theorem-for-success-
b96591bf7dd1

Welch, L. (2022, January 28). *Saving versus investing: Understanding the key differences.* Investopedia. https://www.investopedia.com/articles/investing/0225 16/saving-vs-investing-understanding-key-differences.asp

Westchester gov. (n.d.). *Tips to reduce your debt.* Consumer.westchestergov.com. https://consumer.westchestergov.com/financial-education/credit-and-debt-management/tips-to-reduce-your-debt

Woods, L. (2017, September 11). *10 billionaires like Oprah Winfrey who grew up poor.* CNBC; CNBC. https://www.cnbc.com/2017/09/11/10-billionaires-who-grew-up-dirt-poor.html

Made in the USA
Las Vegas, NV
15 June 2023

73498212R00085